Praise for Lisa C. Uhrik's *America Becoming*

"This is the new lens Americans need in order to see where we are and how we can move forward. The correlations with teenage development and our country's development ring true and give us relatable, shared insight. I'm looking forward to using READ3 as a model and this book as a workbook for facilitating learning and development that transforms individuals, communities, and our country. It's true—as any high school counselor would tell you—the choices we make in this moment will shape the rest of our lives. We are connected, and it is time to make our Declarations of Interdependence."

—Dr. Sharon Cochrane, Literacy, Learning, and Teaching Advocate

"I love this book. At an all-time high of political polarization, Lisa Uhrik cuts through all that divides us to expose who we really are and who we are becoming as a country. An inspiring look into our growing pains and where we can move forward. Read this book and start the conversation envisioned. We are America. And this is not the end, but where we really begin to become."

—Shelley Jared, Attorney, Advocate, and Civil Court Officer

"Incredibly interesting. When I finished reading, I realized I made a Declaration of Interdependence the day I chose to stay and live in my late teens. And since then, I have been seeking revelations and exploration, and I've changed my thinking (and life) entirely. I think reading *America Becoming* could be a game-changer for anyone like me, and that gives me hope. Thank you for writing this book."

—Brianna Patel, Student and Project Specialist

"This book offers us perspective and hope for the possibilities moving forward as a country. I have so enjoyed reading every page and will be looking forward to prompting meaningful discussion with colleagues and friends. Lisa Uhrik has offered us much that is productive here."

—Donna Paz Kaufman, Paz & Associates

"In *America Becoming*, Lisa Uhrik asks us to consider what we think we know to be true and reflect deeply to ask instead 'Do we know how we truly arrived at what we think?' Take this challenge to create a framework for mindset growth, greater perspective, and deeper understanding."

—Bruce Pulver, TEDx Speaker and Author of *Above the Chatter, Our Words Matter*

D1537109

"Taking a look at this country through developmental psychology is new, fresh, and incredibly useful. Lisa Uhrik not only paints a picture that is hopeful, she pulls out a map and shows us how to get someplace better. She shows how to check your game and redirect as a country, for the good of us all."
—Gary Rogers, Christian Influencer and Founder of Check Your Game

"Thank you for writing this. We need this right now. I can't believe how perfect the timing is."
—Joy Watkins, Creative Head, Franklin Fixtures

America Becoming

LISA C. UHRIK, M.ED.

AMERICA BECOMING

Framing Our
Declaration *of* Interdependence

America Becoming
Copyright © 2021 Lisa C. Uhrik
Published by

Southern Fried Karma, LLC
Atlanta, GA
blissfulbeingspress.com

Books are available in quantity for promotional or premium use.
For information, email pr@sfkmultimedia.com.

All Rights Reserved. No part of this book may be reproduced or transmitted in any form
or by any means, electronic or mechanical, including photocopying, recording, or by any
information retrieval or storage system, without the prior written consent of the publisher.

ISBN: 978-1-970137-18-7
eISBN: 978-1-970137-19-4
Library of Congress Control Number available upon request.

Cover & interior design by Olivia Hammerman.
Printed in the United States of America.

For US.
All of us.

Contents

Synopsis

WE'VE BEEN SAYING that America is in trouble for a long time. From almost every corner and political persuasion, we've heard that we are in chaos, in decline, on the verge of disaster.

But what if we're not? What if we're on the verge of something beautiful? What if we're at the precipice of becoming the kind of nation we want to be?

We're in a bit of an identity crisis trying to figure out who exactly we want to be as a nation. In developmental psychology terms, America is one great big teenager. In our toddler years, like all toddlers, we made a Declaration of Independence. As we grew, like most children, we fought. We lost our innocence along the way, and about fifty-five years ago, we entered adolescence as a collective. Egocentric, immortal, loud, proud, irreverent, and obsessively casual in all our ways, we decided to trust no one and have spent an inordinate amount of time taking selfies, trying to figure out who we are.

Today, our mission is to survive America's adolescence without crashing the car, burning down the house, or destroying our reputations. We must also define who we want to be as adults. Will we decide to grow mentally, emotionally, and spiritually? Or will we remain adolescents, trapped in a world of navel-gazing and mistrust? Answering these questions will require us to dig deep, turn inward, embrace dissonance, and learn the adult lessons of interdependence.

Toddlers make declarations of independence and teens live them out. But adults find love, meaning, and connection in Declarations of *Interdependence*.

Dissonance is the stuff of discomfort, confusion, frustration, and uncertainty. And it can be great for us, if we let it. Dissonance can lead to the development and transformation of ourselves and of our relationships. The things that bother us most can lead to a better "us"— individually and collectively.

This book will take you on a journey that is both personal and collective. It will give you a new framework (the READ3 Model) to help you explore four critical phases of intentional development, which are easily pursued to yield transformative insights. The book will end with your being equipped to write your own Declaration of Interdependence for yourself, your family, and your community.

Use this book as:

A path for personal elevation intellectually, emotionally, and spiritually

A framework for graceful, diverse group dialogue and action

A context for reframing and leveraging crisis moments for societal good

Do you want to grow? To make a difference? Do you want to improve your world for yourself and those you love most? By and large, we agree on the difficulties. We see the identity crisis. What we need is something positive—a productive path forward. This book will offer that path.

About the Book's Layout

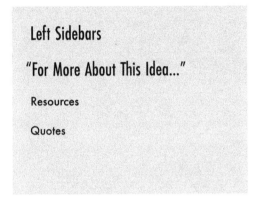

Left Sidebars

"For More About This Idea..."

Resources

Quotes

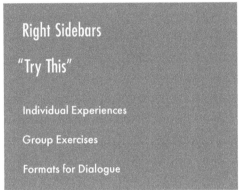

Right Sidebars

"Try This"

Individual Experiences

Group Exercises

Formats for Dialogue

THIS BOOK IS designed to make it easy for you to read, try suggested individual and group exercises, and learn.

Left sidebars offer additional resources, anecdotes, and quotes for thought.

Right sidebars offer individual and group experiences and exercises to choose and use at your pace.

The central text moves from our questions to our developmental context and then into the READ3 Model, outlining a process of personal and group work that leads to writing your own Declaration of Interdependence.

The text shifts focus from considerations for self-development to processes for expanding that development into your community and spheres of influence. We change our world by first changing ourselves.

Chapter 1

How Do I Decide What I Know?

Life seemed a lot easier when our knowing was someone else's job. In our "earlyhoods," things were simpler. We didn't have so many decisions to make. Few people asked for our opinions. In many ways, we trusted that we didn't need to know much. When we had fewer resources for research and learning, life put a lot less pressure on us.

But as we grew—as we learned and saw more of our world—distrust set in.

Our forefathers told us what to think, but we stopped trusting their omnipotence about fifty years ago. Our preachers and teachers gave us a script until their feet of clay led us to eye even the most well-intended and dedicated among them with suspicion.

Our heroes in entertainment gave us models of lives to aspire to, but we have since discerned that they are only sparkled-up versions of us and therefore suspect. Now, when our legislators speak, we mostly devalue and discard the partisan banter that has drowned out the original model of democratic debate.

We trusted the media and then found that we are the media, with little interest in cloaking our biases. We have cameras and microphones and an ability to call in "the news" from any location at any time to our personal readership; our followers on Twitter, Facebook, or Instagram; or our personal contacts. This capacity was only a glimmer of what it is now a decade ago, and it was virtually unheard of twenty years ago. We have become the loudest sources of news in America. It is ironic that we call news fake because we create most of the information that we see and believe.

Try This: Finding Space to Think

Exercise in personal thinking:

1. Name one space you can go now where you are free to think and speak, even just to yourself.
2. Go there.
3. As in meditation, give yourself twenty minutes to just be and think. Let your mind flow.
4. After twenty minutes, record your thoughts in some way: a journal, an audio recording, etc.
5. Now read them back. Listen to yourself for a moment. What do you hear? What do you feel?

This space is just for you sorting you.

It doesn't take longer than a good workout or an episode of some show—think of it as today's gift to you. And it needs to be today, if at all possible. The energy you gain in giving yourself this moment will be fuel for the rest of today's moments.

And so we are left with only ourselves. It's no wonder that we are having such a hard time knowing what we think.

So how do we decide what we think?

Most of us are familiar with Descartes's proclamation "I think, therefore I am." But fewer of us know the full version of his message: *dubito, ergo cogito, ergo sum.*[1] *I doubt, therefore I think, therefore I am.* It turns out that all of this doubt is terribly useful in determining what we believe and who we are (our identity). The suspicion is what psychologists and others call dissonance, because it is like a musical chord in us that doesn't resolve. It feels uncomfortable, and the urge to work it out is intense.

We need to talk about our doubts and our dissonance. But where do we speak our niggling doubts and potential heresies?

Space to unpack our collected thoughts and decide which to keep is one of the rarest—and most precious—things we can find or cultivate. But instead of seeking dissonance and inviting doubt, we gravitate to puddles of agreement, because those feel safer than speaking a half-considered thought into the deep end of the public pool of anger, hurt, or insensitivity.

Where can we go to embrace this doubt and dissonance? Where do we have the freedom to pick up ideas and put them down again? We can browse the internet, sure, but that doesn't entirely scratch this intellectual itch. This need runs deep and requires that we have space not just to listen but to speak. Trying on ideas by saying them out loud or writing them is essential to our becoming. And with internet algorithms mowing neat rows for our paradigm-reinforcing perusal, it's tough to get out of our own mental lane. It's easy to operate under the illusion that everyone sees the same thing as us when they log on to their computer or device. But more and more, the power of algorithms shapes what we see. In every form of technology we touch—from emails and internet searches to social-media suggestions and ads to the phones in our palms—we are fed ideas, articles, information, clothing, memes, cartoons, opinion pieces, news, and even friends who reinforce our own fledgling views.

This creates an echo chamber, giving us a cocooning illusion that the rest of the world agrees with us. We find this comfortable, which the engineers behind these algorithms know—it's part of what pulls us back to their platforms again and again. In the echo chamber, we don't have to be experts, because the algorithm agrees with our first thoughts and reinforces them with an abundance of hard evidence. You've experienced it—that eerie feeling that someone is inside your head. How did the internet magically know that you wanted a garden bench? How did your phone know you were trying to lose weight? Why are you suddenly receiving emails about decorating your bedroom? But the power of these algorithms extends beyond our diets and decorating senses. Increasingly, they shape our worldviews, our political beliefs, and our desires for our community and family. Suddenly, changing the way we think looks extremely dangerous.

Our private musings are reinforced so heavily that they become a box of sorts. We become stuck inside our secret, and now intractable, paradigms, which are at the root of our personal and collective educational dilemmas today.

A few years ago, a neighbor posted a yellow sign on area trees about our city's lake: "Save our lake. It is dying!" Soon there were T-shirts, yard signs, and organization meetings. I saw it so often that I believed it must be true, so my mental box became "Our city lake (on which we have property) is dying." I began to see all the things in the lake that reinforced that lens: a concerning-seeming number of snapping turtles and carp, sludge, and mud. It seemed that the whole neighborhood was

in agreement. But then at some point, the question occurred to me: How do we know that there is a problem here? Where is the analysis, the data, the research? Finding none, I started looking for the opposite view—the idea that our city lake was progressing naturally.

Interestingly, I never made a single public statement about my view on our city lake—at least consciously. But with my changed perspective, as with my initial one, I found a host of neighbors and friends who agreed. My social media was flooded with angry realtors and homeowners and even a questioning wildlife and fisheries person or two saying that the lake was mostly fine.

Then, one night recently, a friend asked my husband Dave and me, "Isn't the lake in trouble?" and my honest answer was, "I have no idea." Even after the efforts of a few years, I am left with two polarized views and little that helps me know what I think.

This happens every day with just about every concern we carry, and it is damaging our ability to know what to think and to take productive action.

So what are we to do? How do we escape this echo chamber? Where do we go to truly listen to an idea from a different paradigm or culture? How do we invite the doubt Descartes speaks of?

Mental Scaffolding Needed

You've likely picked up this book because you're the kind of person who pays attention. You want to move, personally and collectively, toward better ways of being. In life, play, work, and love, you recognize that this moment is ripe for finding and framing some different sorts of declarations. You are not alone. To make room for new ideas, we need some mental scaffolds. Mental scaffolds are not that different from the ones you see on buildings as they go up. To erect a new space for anything (psychological or physical), you need scaffolding to allow you to climb up to another level where you can see more. From there, you can work on that new level before walking on it.

If someone told you about a rare bird in a part of the world you knew nothing about, you wouldn't be likely to retain much of the lesson. If someone gave you complex information about tax law and you knew little about taxes, you'd lose that piece of information quickly.

If someone gave you a long string of random numbers—say 1050220202021, for example—you'd have little likelihood of being able to remember them, right? (Didn't your eyes just pass over those numbers in a nice skim?)

Let's say that there is a $100 bill waiting for you if you remember those numbers. Even then, that's going to be hard, right? But if you had a scaffold for those numbers—an understanding of their meaning and order—you'd be able to create a framework and use that to remember the number set.

To demonstrate, let's say:

1 = the first number in the series

05 02 2020 = the date this section was written

2021 = the year this book was published

With that mental scaffold, it would be easy to recall 1 05 02 2020 2021.

Whether we are conscious of it or not, we use scaffolds for everything we do and learn. They give us something to stand on, to hang things on, and space from which we can work on a new task, idea, or thing. There are many things in our lives today that need new frameworks to grow—and we need a little privacy to put the frame together.

This is where the framing of our interdependence begins: the realization that we need the push and pull of others to help us determine our actions through our doubts. We need someone to hold up philosophical poles on the other sides of the tent so that we can see what is under the canopy between the flagpole we hold and those different perspectives.

In other words, we need someone to say an idea that is really different from our own and look at the truth in between the two ideas. Position one: the lake is dying. Position two: the lake is in great shape. We need dialogue to understand each of those perspectives and the truths in between them.

The way we argue, you'd think we were doing big things. But mostly, we're not. Why do we feel compelled to have such strong opinions about things over which we have so little direct influence?

Finding a Productive Space to Learn

For the last decade or more, we have relied on social media as a trusted—even "local"—source to help us decide what we think. But even as we pull in the new friends that seem likely to reinforce our worldview, we discover that there are differences even within our self-selected pools. Our security in what we think and say erodes. Voice the "wrong thing" on social media, and you may find yourself verbally pummeled with the heat of a thousand suns. No wonder so many of us feel isolated.

We demand show-me-your-everything transparency and authenticity and then offer no flexibility when such naked revelations fall outside "acceptable" boundaries. In an article for *The Atlantic* in 2020, Yuval Levin noted that a lack of privacy in the quest for transparency has seemingly created an unintended consequence everywhere, even in our Congress: "Too many have just one mode—a performative mode intended to go viral. And in that mode, Congress cannot function."[2]

Congress cannot function, and we personally cannot grow, in these fishbowls we've created. We need some space to discuss, to be wrong, to say things in flawed ways without becoming (hilarious) memes competing with cute animals and sassy children for public attention. We need the same things that a baby needs when learning to stand: leverage—something to push against—and purpose—something to reach. We also need muscles that cooperate—a type of mental control—and an environment that allows us to fall without getting hurt.

Social media has become, quite definitely, not that productive space. We read something. We agree. Or we vehemently disagree. We feel like joining a dialogue could be useful. And it absolutely is—some of the time. But often, what we're experiencing is a discussion, not a conversation.

Discussion is an exciting word. It shares the same root as *percussion*: "*quatere*: to shake or to shake up." We can interpret this figuratively as batting words like one would take a stick to a drum. I beat my drum; you beat yours. Sometimes we have a drum corps, and that sounds wonderful. Sometimes we all agree and just pontificate and beat our drums in alignment. We may each be very singular in our perspectives or views, but it feels good to find that alignment, to be in rhythm with others. We scan social media for folks who will affirm our position, agree with us, and help us settle into our own mental easy chairs.

But when we don't find alignment, the art of our social media and text discussions is more like a drum contest. We are batting ideas *at* each other, and the one with the most sensational beat wins. There's a mic drop—done.

We pay lip service in our culture to the importance of dialogue, but I'm not sure we often find good dialogue in the wilds of America today. Dialogue involves a building of understandings, precept on precept. Dialogue is a molded position, not a fixed one that is batted about. What we offer the world today most often are monologues, not dialogues. Dialogue involves having the space to think about what we believe… to doubt and to discover.

That's what we're after here in this book. It's why I wrote it. I want to give you a space to doubt, to think, to find your revelations, and to frame your thoughts.

From "Free Bird" to "Better Together": Discussion to Dialogue

When we were a toddler nation, we framed our developmental space as a Declaration of Independence. It was a discussion beat on a drum heard 'round the world. As a teenage nation, we've stretched every chord of that first independent song to its dramatic limits.

The song "Free Bird" is an exemplary anthem for a teenage nation. Singing in full voice, we joined Lynyrd Skynyrd as free birds that cannot change.[3]

But if we've lived a few years, we understand that freedom changes as we grow older, doesn't it?

It's time to replace "Free Bird" with a new anthem. Because really, how free are you if you wail that you cannot change?

The reality is that this bird (you, me, and all of us) can change. Not only can we change, but change, in fact, is the very nature of things. Things change or they die. Change is the only constant. Wittingly or unwittingly, we are always on the move. The question is, how much are we paying attention from behind the wheel as we journey?

"Better Together" by Jack Johnson seems a better anthem for this moment.[4] Working with each other and with the benefit of real dialogue, we can refine our own thinking rather than becoming prey to the created forces of social media and algorithms that unwittingly shape us. In the safety-tension of togetherness, we can move through our questions. We can grow faith. We can move through fear and doubt. And, in the best ways, we have the potential to refine ourselves with the help of others.

It's not easy to wrest the wheel from the invisible-reinforcement armies, but together, it is possible. Deciding what we think is, after all, core to our Declaration of Independence and the original framing of America.

American Anger

The way we argue in this country, you'd think we were doing big things. All over America today, there are living-room, conference-room, social-media, and dinette debates filled with exceptionally intense emotions. We could be discussing politics, school, disease, jobs, faith, sports, or dog training. No matter the topic, American conversations today are colored with passion. But not much is actually happening with all that heat.

No one can tell you what you should do. But, please, do take the wheel in your own journey.

From birth, humans throw tantrums when frustrated. They just look different as we grow.

Digging Under Your Anger: A Personal Exercise

Four simple questions can help us see the point about our own strong opinions and evaluate where we sit on the frustration spectrum:

1. Name the last three times you sounded angry.
2. What was the subtext of that anger (the feeling of fear or pain behind the mask of anger)?
3. Did you curse or show your emotions in another way?
4. What was your desired outcome for that conversation?

Write the answers down, not to reinforce your anger or relive the experiences, but to set them apart from you and examine them for a moment.

And leave them alone for now.

On a recent shopping trip before a nephew's wedding, my husband Dave and I encountered a sales clerk that left a strong impression. Mary was in her late eighties and all of five feet tall. My husband, looking for a new suitcoat, found something quickly and at a steal. Mary approved: "That's going to wear on you well. Good fit. And it's a great price." Pleased with his lightning-fast bargain suitcoat selection, Dave beamed at her compliment, and the three of us struck up a brief conversation. I helped as we talked by holding the hanger as Mary's arthritic hands pulled the bag over the coat. At eighty-six years of age, Mary told us she had worked in the department store for three decades. A self-proclaimed expert in men's apparel, Mary said she studied her customers closely. We asked what she had observed in her thirty years in the department store. She paused. "Well, most people won't talk, like you all." She paused and leaned in, as though in fear of unsettling someone. "People are just so… very…angry."

I was profoundly struck by Mary's comment. Immediately, my mind flooded with thoughts of the recent violence and tragedies in the news. I thought of the young gunman at the garlic festival in California shouting, "I'm just outraged."[5] I thought, too, of the rising suicide rates, as suicide often is a form of anger turned inward. I thought of school shootings and violence in churches.

Anger.

There are many such acts of violence driven by anger each year in America.

Why are people so angry? From social-media diatribes to violent outbursts to reflections of the emotion in our comedy, we Americans seem an angry lot. What's at the root of this?

Anger, fear, sadness, loss, and love. Our tears flow when we don't have words big enough for our emotions. Similarly, our feelings seem to flow when we don't know what we think or why we think it. We are caught in a tangle of thoughts. The frustration becomes overwhelming. We see injustice and then question what we see. We hear a perspective and then find it immediately refuted. We take a mental—or physical—stand only to find the ground shaking beneath our feet.

From birth, humans throw tantrums when frustrated. They just look different as we grow. I believe that this generalized anger is part of our—often painful—growth as a country today.

And while that may seem a hopeless thing, I see it as a transitional one. I believe that our frustration while sorting out our tangled thoughts and our inability to sort through all of the information coming at us helps explain our heated debates across the country: We have red-hot opinions about things over which we have little direct influence because our thoughts exist in frustrating tangles.

You've experienced this: You're sitting at a table filled with heat and emotion—maybe you're talking about politics, race, the NFL, a Netflix special, or healthcare. You've found yourself wondering, "What's going on? Why are we talking about this? And what has informed the passion in this discussion?"

There's a lot of noise, isn't there? Mary was right—people are just so angry.

We are angry because we are in a confusing part of our development. Like an adolescent assaulted by hormones and countless thoughts, our country is dining on a confusion burger with a super-sized side of anger. But anger is not a root emotion. It is a mask for vulnerable core emotions. According to psychologist Richard Roberts:

Behavioral scientists have conducted numerous experimental studies on the emotions of anger and fear. However, despite volumes of data, most of them have missed the key element in the relationship between the two emotional states: anger almost always masks fear (or some sort of "weaker," more vulnerable emotion, such as anxiety, shame, guilt, helplessness, or grief).[6]

On Cursing

Have you noticed that we curse a lot these days? This reflects America's passion.

Swear words are special in our brains. Cursing is an emotional language, tapping into that part of the brain between words and art. People who experience strokes often find themselves cursing uncharacteristically. Curse words flow from an instinctive part of the brain and express an intensity of emotion—perhaps because we can't find other words sufficient to get these feelings across.

Cursing is rooted in the limbic system, a collection of deep-brain regions responsible for processing emotions, certain automatic drives and habits, and even aspects of learning. Swearing has an undeniable emotional component—some scientists argue that swearing is more about expressing an emotional state than articulating an actual linguistic idea.[7]

To Ponder:

Does cursing help you in dialogue or take the conversation in different directions?

If/when you curse, are you aware of the shift away from cognition into emotion? Do you lose the conversation or keep it going with cursing?

A Path Out of Anger and Toward Growth

What is our path forward out of this diet of anger? I believe the expression of anger has a lot to do with this core truth: We are trying to decide what we think, and to do that, we need to get our thoughts out of our heads and hearts and look at them. We need to hold our pole of thought while others keep theirs, and we need to look at all of those ideas to assess the truth.

Our emotions' strength does not invalidate our positions' logic. We need to express both our reason and our feelings while keeping the dialogue open. Only when we can get all our thoughts out and listen, look, and evaluate can we decide what we want to carry with us. Only then can we become authentic about the root of our anger—our grief, our fear, our hope, or our frustration.

Ben Franklin had a model for deciding what he thought that he captured in his autobiography. Hundreds of years later, it feels timely and relevant. Franklin wrote that when he was twenty-three, he noted his own need to frame his thoughts and manage his life with a personal framework of belief. He discerned his need for a system to guide his daily action and selected endeavors. Franklin put together a set of thirteen virtues by which he wanted to live. These were the topics that he wanted to know more about—these were the subjects that he wanted to study deeply and about which he tried to make thoughtful decisions.

But that list was just the start of sorting through his thoughts. His next construct was one that we perhaps need more than anything else today. After putting together his thirteen virtues, Franklin gathered some diverse folks—friends, frenemies, and a couple of people he didn't know very well at all—and invited them on a journey. The journey's goal was to continually refine their own thinking, pushing against each other's diverse perspectives and pulling one another forward by the desire for personal improvement and the opportunity to contribute something useful to their families and society.

The space that Franklin created in 1727 has enormous utility for us today. He called it the Leather Apron Club, and the group referred to themselves as a "junto" (from "junta," which is Spanish for assembly).[8] The club's twelve members were drawn from diverse occupations, including printers, surveyors, cabinetmakers, clerks, and bartenders. They shared a spirit of inquiry and a desire to improve themselves, improve their community, and help others. Though Franklin was likely the youngest among them, he was also the leader of their weekly meetings.

In his autobiography, Franklin details the key to this group's success. Their purpose was twofold in each meeting: 1) to identify an action the member would take to improve himself and 2) to determine an action the member would take to improve their world.

Note this critical piece: the meetings were not about persuading one another to a point of view or way of thinking, but about framing individual explorations and actions. Those personal explorations came from the revelations—the "aha" moments—of listening "without a fondness for dispute or desire for victory,"[9] as Franklin put it. Direct contradictions were made contraband in the group.

The group met weekly, more or less, for forty-four years. And out of their meetings, great things were born. The public library system was formed. The volunteer fire department was created. In fact, most of the great initiatives attributed to Franklin's life can be traced back in one way or another to this self-improvement group dialogue.[10]

It seems rational that a little private, focused conversation could do some good for us too. There's an organization called the Franklin Circle that continues this work today in New York. Their motto is, "Transform your life. Transform your world." They offer free resources on how any individual can start their own Franklin Circle.

Compelled by the model, I started a Franklin Circle a couple of years ago, and it was terrific. (I say "was" because life got in the way, and we have let this good thing lapse.) But for the ten months that we pursued it, transformative things happened in each group member's life. One participant reunited her family thanks to the exercise of Franklin's thirteen virtues, another found herself significantly less angry at work, and I found the impetus to write down these thoughts that have been swirling around for a decade. You're reading them now, in part, because of a Franklin Circle. (As I write, I'm compelled to renew this group effort, and I recognize that it helped shape everything from household organization to community initiatives for me.)

Our group was respectful, engaging, and interested, but even as I write that it was "life" that got in the way, I suspect something more complicated was afoot. I think I reached an impasse that I haven't quite found a way through. I found it challenging to steer and guide the conversation from pontifications on beliefs to personal commitments and actions. I think that's because as a society, right now, we're looking for likes. It is to that idea—looking for "likes" and agreement—that I'd like to turn next.

Looking for Likes or "Unlikes"

Developmental psychology tells us that there are two primary ways to leverage others' thoughts in the formation of our own perspectives: alignment and differentiation. *Someone thinks like me. Someone thinks differently than me.* It seems simple. But behind each process are two powerful forces at play, each rooted in different needs, and those needs are critical to our growth.

Alignment—appreciation of how we are similar—is rooted in the feminine part of our personalities. Differentiation and hierarchy—appreciation of how we are different—are rooted in our personalities' masculine part. As we seek to understand the formation of our personal perspectives—deciding what we think—it helps to first understand our own preferences. Do you tend to look for likes and commonalities as you move and grow? Or do you find it most helpful to see your differences and how your path is unique?

It is important to note that, though I've used the terms "feminine" and "masculine" here, these preferences do not have to divide along gender lines. For example, Ben Franklin's group seems a unique blend of the masculine and feminine in development (though it is recorded as only involving men). The model of the Franklin Circle[11] is one we'll explore in more depth later alongside other improvement-dialogue groups, like book clubs and Socratic groups. Still, it is interesting that the Franklin structure[12] seems to allow for traditionally masculine and traditionally feminine "voices" and developmental needs.

In her well-known work studying young girls, *In a Different Voice,* Carol Gilligan[13] documented how young feminine identities are primarily formed by girls learning what they have in common with other girls. (Gilligan defined "girl" as a young female between the ages of eight and fifteen.) Gilligan found that girls frequently use the word "like" in conversation and identified this as a normative, female-centric way of creating alignment— literally. "I'm like you; you're like me."

When someone is thinking like me, agreeing with me, or enjoying something that I like, I experience a sort of safety and confirmation. Collaborating or supporting someone is an indirect way of defending oneself. Those imitating a young female voice often use the word "like" a great deal. "I was, like, so impressed with that speech because it, like, really spoke to my situation." Sometimes, the infusions of "like" are associated with immaturity. But Gilligan helps us see that using the word "like" is

> I draw on the work of Piaget (1968) in identifying conflict as the harbinger of growth and also on the work of Erikson (1964) who, in charting development through crisis, demonstrates how a heightened vulnerability signals the emergence of a potential strength, creating a dangerous opportunity for growth, "a turning point for better or worse" (p. 139).
>
> —CAROL GILLIGAN,
> *In a Different Voice: Psychological Theory and Women's Development*

not about insecurity or weakness. It is about seeking commonality upon which to build. Gilligan's findings paint a picture of what she identifies as a uniquely feminine approach to development: learning how we are alike and different helps one refine one's definitions of self. So, finding a kindred spirit is like finding a set of scaffolds: now you can climb and hang things; now you can work on building your understandings.

Isn't it interesting how much of our social media has formed around this concept of "liking" things? The idea, documented as being necessary to the feminine developmental process, has become core to every sort of social, business, and societal movement.

The male developmental characteristic traditionally identified with young boys is that they find their identities through separation, competition, and hierarchy. Competition and order are not just the stuff of play, but of understanding oneself.

While I cite these studies to suggest that in our culture, at this moment, young girls and young boys seek their identities on the whole through different processes, increasingly, developmental research supports that each of us is a distinct blend of the feminine and masculine archetypes and needs. The point is that different types of situations and dynamics help us decide what we think. For some, it is the power of someone with a similar perspective. For others, it is the power to possess a standout idea that sets them apart, or the ability to win. These are some of the ways we decide what it is that we know. It's helpful to know which matters more to you—alignment with others, having commonalities and "likes," or having a unique idea and your own brand of thought. Personal awareness of that preference is helpful as you talk with others.

And regardless of your preference, we all use the power of conversation to either align or differentiate ourselves. We are looking for ways to decide what we know and trust. And in that quest (as any Bluetooth device will tell you multiple times a day), "We are connected."

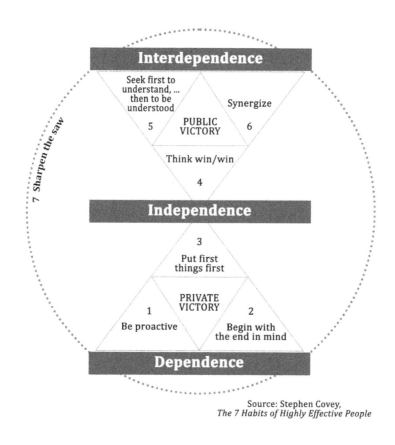

Source: Stephen Covey,
The 7 Habits of Highly Effective People

Our Next Step—A Quest for Interdependence

Connected. Have you noticed how often that word is part of our world today? It's our theme song in America. While perhaps the tune is familiar, we couldn't tell you the gist of the song or its import. That word is most salient here because it reflects the higher state of wisdom and spiritual understanding that is our developmental task to achieve as a country today.

American educator and businessman Stephen Covey's beloved book *The 7 Habits of Highly Effective People*[14] telegraphs the journey to effectiveness as the movement from "me" to "we." According to Covey, the journey to "we" begins with self-mastery—working on and with yourself—and the private victories of setting a course, having a personal end in mind, organizing oneself and one's life around that vision, and having control over our impulses. That can happen with others or independently, in alignment or in differentiation, but all of the discomfort and dissonance associated with that first stage of growth is about "me."

As we'll explore, America has been highly invested in this independent journey to "me," with incredible (if not entirely consistent) results.

But as Covey puts it, "Life is, by nature, highly interdependent. To try to achieve maximum effectiveness through independence is like trying to play tennis with a golf club."[15] And that may be precisely what we're trying to do these days as a country—play a little tennis with a golf club. No wonder we're so frustrated and angry! Our social media screams our independence and our quests for living our best lives, but we can't actually do that alone.

Dependent people need others to get what they want. Independent people can get what they want through their own effort. Interdependent people combine their efforts with the efforts of others. And while we want to improve our interdependent systems in our communities and country, Covey asserts that "You cannot continuously improve interdependent systems and processes until you progressively perfect interdependent, interpersonal relationships."[16]

This topmost level of work and living—interdependence—is a choice only independent people can make. Interdependence is a state of wisdom and spiritual awareness that many never reach. It is a space where you realize you are not the center of the universe. We recognize in that state that any wisdom we have does not come *from* us but flows *through* us. When we move from perspectives pulled straight out of our navels toward seeing others' perspectives and using those to decide what we really believe, something essential shifts.

Let's unpack interdependence just a little more. Interdependence encompasses the ways my health is dependent on your decisions (from pollution to viruses to secondhand smoke). It can mean the ways that a small-business owner is hanging on my willingness to shop locally or the ways that our city park is connected to the taxes that business owners will pay out of that income.

Lest we think such high-minded notions are beyond our grasp, look around, and you'll see that we've got this, at least in some fundamental ways. When you're really discouraged by society, think about the miracle of interdependence that happens every time you get into the car and drive on a city street or interstate. Drivers from age 15 to 105 with questionable personal decision-making skills and wildly varying moods and worldviews share the road every day. And they do it mainly without incident—all behind the wheels of massive machines capable of dizzying speeds.

It is a miracle of interdependence, and it reflects that we are capable of great cooperative acts.

Let's Shift from:
"Live Your Best Life"
to
"Live Our Best Lives."

Interdependence is the good stuff. I'm reminded that before any declarations of

Try This: Start Your Journey by Creating A Franklin Circle

Want to change the world like Ben Franklin did? Explore the idea of the Franklin Circle at https://benfranklincircles.org/.[17]

Here's how it works if you want to start one:

1. Pick a diverse membership. In 1727, Franklin formed the Junto (from the Spanish word for assembly), a weekly mutual-improvement club made up of individuals with an array of interests and skills. Diversity of belief, experience, culture, and worldview is like the placement of poles for a tent: the wider the span of difference, the more ideas that can live underneath it. It's challenging to be in the presence of someone whose thoughts are wildly different, but if you can connect through a chosen set of values, as Franklin has arranged, there is much to be gained—much that you don't know you don't know. And isn't that the best way to grow?

2. Find the right place and time and meet for a couple of hours at regular intervals (weekly, monthly). You'll need a few minutes to settle in, to look at each other and catch up, with the balance of the first hour spent on reviewing the actions taken toward improvement since the last meeting. The second hour will be spent talking about the next virtue as a topic, with the aim of identifying more actions.

3. Create a space conducive to communication and invite members. The space should be quiet enough to hear each other in a group without shouting and small enough to feel human-scale and safe (like a corner, a living room, a small conference room at the library, or a book-club table at a local bookstore.)

4. Use guidelines to set the parameters for a call to action regarding one of the virtues each time you meet. Decide on "one action I will take to improve myself; one action I will take to improve my world."

The action-oriented approach is the root of self-improvement, and the goal of the dialogue is not to agree or to argue, but to be expanded through dialogue toward new thoughts and chosen actions.

Founding Father Ben Franklin was, among other things, a pioneer of self-improvement.

love, before we'd ever touched hands, Dave spoke across his desk and said without pre-amble, "I've heard that every pot needs its lid. And you're mine." Huh? Though un-spoken love simmered between us on high, I didn't see it. But because I respected him so much, I looked again and realized how much I appreciated the metaphor. If you're going to cook something exceptional, you need interdependence. There's nothing like a good pot and lid, and it doesn't really matter what name you give the individual parts—the interdependent whole is where the secret sauce marinates.

It's an exciting thought that we're on the verge of delicious growth as a coun-try. After watching the Broadway show *Hamilton* in an election year, I read the Declaration of Independence top to bottom. And I was amazed at the inter-dependent concepts framing it. We had to move from dependence to independence in those first 240 years. But we're just on the cusp of claiming interdependence as our next great space of development. The present dissonance of our world today—politically, socially, economically, environ-mentally, physically—and the vulnerability and associated mask of anger that come with it do not spell the end of democracy but its fulfillment. George Washington, Ben Franklin, and the other framers set up an elegantly interdependent system through our government and the Electoral College. That interdependence impacts us every day in many ways we rarely reflect on, even as we drive together.

We are on the cusp: ripe for developing out of climactic crises and into a better US.

We can choose to use our dissonance while moving along the developmental path—while growing. And human development has a lot to teach us about how to facilitate that growth individually and collectively.

To understand where we are develop-mentally and where we'd ultimately like to go, let's back up and get some context about how we got here.

Chapter 2

America in 240 Years: From Toddler to Teen

We Are Here

| identity | intimacy | generativity | ego-integrity |

basic trust   autonomy   initiative   industry   identity   intimacy   generativity   ego-integrity

INFANT   TODDLER   PRE-SCHOOLER   SCHOOL-AGER   ADOLESCENT   YOUNG ADULT   MIDDLE AGE   OLDER ADULT

basic mistrust   shame & doubt   guilt   inferiority   role confusion   isolation   stagnation   despair

WHEN AMERICA WAS a toddler, she carried that red, white, and blue blanket Aunt Betsy made everywhere. She hung on to every word her Founding Fathers wrote and thought them wise and wonderful. She loved her name and her home, and she enjoyed imagining her future.

When she was a child, she had some big fights with her brother—and there were household casualties all over the place. But eventually, they united against the big bullies from across the pond, and while it was a loss of innocence and an age of learning reason for her, those victories seemed to draw America's whole family closer.

When America was a toddler, she carried that red, white, and blue blanket Aunt Betsy made everywhere.

In her preteen years, she enjoyed expanding her interests and was serious about her studies. She went to church, dressed neatly, and worked on small-town development projects. She made pen-pal friends around the world and relished her time with family. She put a note in a bottle and sent it into space, dreamy-eyed about the stars.

A decade or so before her two-hundredth birthday, America hit puberty. Suddenly, her forefathers didn't sound very smart, and she started questioning, well, *everything.* She became more vocal about her views, became more radical in the way she dressed, and turned her music up loud. She experimented with sex and drugs and felt a rush of feelings she didn't quite understand.

Over the past few decades, America, known mostly by the nickname USA, has been a full-fledged set of teenagers. We have been more likely to have watched an Alec Baldwin skit than to be able to name our senators and representatives. We haven't cared who owned the car as long as we had the keys at the ready for a drive. We've been immortal, eating and drinking without a care for the future.

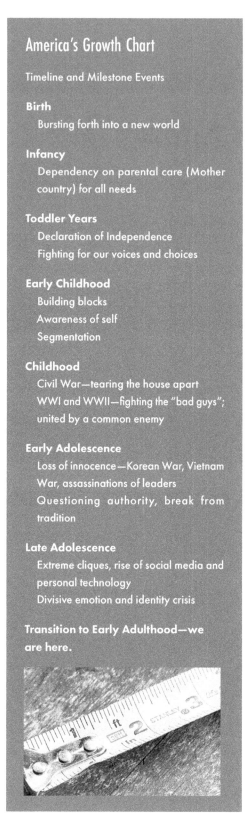

America's Growth Chart

Timeline and Milestone Events

Birth
   Bursting forth into a new world

Infancy
   Dependency on parental care (Mother country) for all needs

Toddler Years
   Declaration of Independence
   Fighting for our voices and choices

Early Childhood
   Building blocks
   Awareness of self
   Segmentation

Childhood
   Civil War—tearing the house apart
   WWI and WWII—fighting the "bad guys"; united by a common enemy

Early Adolescence
   Loss of innocence—Korean War, Vietnam War, assassinations of leaders
   Questioning authority, break from tradition

Late Adolescence
   Extreme cliques, rise of social media and personal technology
   Divisive emotion and identity crisis

Transition to Early Adulthood—we are here.

Try This:

Pull out a pen or pencil and a piece of paper (something different happens when we write with our hands) and write yourself a "dear diary" note.

Dear Diary,

Here's the question that keeps rolling through my mind right now:

Who am I now?

Who do I want to become?

How do I sort this out?

Love, America

We've been egocentric, certain that the world is orbiting around us and making a study of our every move. We've been cliquish and have had perhaps a wee bit of an inflated view of our own capabilities. We've remained scintillated by news of sex or scandal. We've divided the class into devoted friends and fierce enemies. And our paranoia has grown along with our drug problem, as both seem to be getting worse even as I write this.[18]

We can tell you everything about the hottest person with the most followers in class but little about the needs of our neighborhoods, much less the needs of our neighbors around the world. We've dropped our global pen-pals and trained our gaze on the mirror, where we've admired our perfect white teeth and worked on today's selfie smile. We've amassed long lists of friends—but they have been surface-level, cliquish friends who reinforced our worldviews. We have used the word "like" a whole lot. We've developed a language of symbols and letters to express our high emotions. It's hard to imagine our texts and tweets would be decipherable to the Founding Fathers. They would be horrified at the deterioration of America's language and the kinds of things we say about others. And they would wonder why we sign everything with an "LOL."

We'd tell them that it means "laughing out loud," which seems ironic, as we haven't been laughing a lot, these days. The question "Who am I?" has been heavy on the mind of this United teen. Like for any teen, our crisis of identity feels all-consuming as America struggles to find a way to describe her family, and she doesn't want to be boxed into any one definition of self. Such struggles produce a general state of dissonance mid-self-discovery. We've been up and down with heavy swings, and suicide has become a common part of our national experience. We have had violent outbursts that we can't explain, and we've become a bit cynical. We don't believe anything or anyone anymore. Even our own social circles are viewed with peppered cynicism.

Mother Nature has had a furrow in her brow. She's given her USA so much and in return has been wounded. America seems blind to the riches and gifts in her home. Mother Nature keeps offering nutrition, but America chooses fast food, prescriptions, and opioids for fuel.

As America embraces late adolescence, things are shifting a little.

Maturational Development

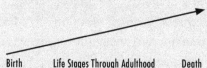

Birth   Life Stages Through Adulthood   Death

Using Erik Erikson's[19] views of the natural stages we experience as we mature, we find ourselves just a wee bit right of the center point as a country. It took us 240 years to get to this point, which means it's likely that, at least in maturational terms, we have yet to hit our middle age as a country.

Great news! We're still young!

Better news: we have some important decisions to make.

Try This

Big, Big, Big Thought Question:

How would I describe the kind of society that I would like to see and the kind of life that I would like to have?

We are by turns highly productive
and easily bored, and we binge on
entertainment like we used to love
on ice cream.

We've moved from giggling, tantalized whispers about sex to in-your-face sexual obsession to extreme sexual exploration to perhaps a more integrated view of sex and self.

If you want to get America's attention, you can still give us a tweet about sex, retaining our youth (or hair), or losing weight. Our attention span remains short—so keep your words and characters in line, or we'll swipe left.

We have a need for speed—fix this now—and easy entertainment. We are by turns highly productive and easily bored, and we binge on entertainment like we used to love on ice cream.

America's new blanket isn't the red, white, and blue one in her room, but a protective case on a phone. No stuffed animal from our childhood could compete with the consistent intensity with which we carry our phones.

As long as we have battery power, we're okay, but without it, we feel as lost as last year's Easter egg. In a true gesture of intimacy, we'll let you hold our phone for a moment…maybe five seconds. But after five seconds, we get jittery and need it back. Like, now.

Even in late adolescence, America is loud and proud and full of energy that by turns fascinates and annoys our aunts and uncles around the globe. We often make them laugh, even when this is not our intent.

Our biggest contribution to our world may be that we are innovative and entertaining. We think everyone wants to be us, and while that's not exactly true, it is true that others are drawn seemingly inexhaustibly to our open ways and freedoms. And they all love to watch and listen to the art we make. We don't just seek entertainment at every turn, we lead the globe in manufacturing it. We're sensational in expression. Our yearbook is full of signatures and pictures. Our social-media accounts (a yearbook of sorts for the twenty-first century) have ballooned to tomes that could fill even the biggest library. We record and report everything about our lives, from the plate of pancakes to the wall in a random restroom, certain that many will find it fascinating. We'll know, because we measure success through the dopamine hit of likes and shares.

We follow sports like politics and politics like sports and wear our team colors in every post. Most of us treat it almost as a duty to make it clear which side we're on. This can be a positive thing, as we're willing to work hard for our team. But it can easily become negative, as we lose ourselves to heated debates, feeding our rage.

Very recently, we've drawn in close to our crew. We do vacations and dances and extras with family. We seem to be genuinely looking for a little good news and wise leadership. We want to know who to listen to; we're searching for good models to help us craft who we will become.

And like any teenager with a license to drive, we need to figure out how to navigate these years without burning down the house, wrecking the car, or ruining our reputation. As an older nation might tell us, the choices we make today will shape the adult nation that we will become.

All this evidence links America's developmental path with human developmental paths. That's why I offer that we're in a transitional stage of development as a country today. We are occupying that space between late adolescence and young adulthood where our choices matter a lot. And at least some part of us seems aware of that, though we haven't yet put these particular words to it.

There's a name for where we are: late adolescence. And there's a name for where we're immediately headed through our trips around the sun: young adulthood.

It's important to recognize that the growth that occurs as we move into our young adulthood happens in two ways: with and without our intention.

In the following pages, we will explore both, starting with the growth milestones that happen whether or not we want them to. After that, we'll spend some time unpacking the kind of growth that happens by choice.

Together, over the course of these pages, we're headed toward crafting our own Declaration of Interdependence, which is most certainly an intentional sort of mission.

To get to that interdependent space, I've created an appropriate acronym to describe the developmental process called "READ3." I say "appropriate" because reading is a key that unlocks several of the steps of our developmental process. While READ3 outlines an intentional growth process for you as an individual, I believe it also applies to us as a country. Because individual change and collective change—as Ben Franklin's little junto would tell you—are inextricably linked.

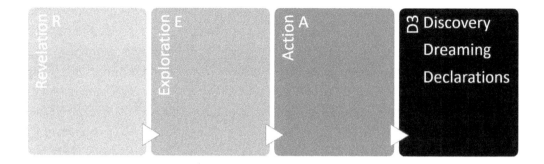

As a developmental counselor, I'm prepared to help an individual move forward through the life stages involved in being human. A counselor helps a person feeling stuck or in crisis find the stepping stones to growth. Think of the balance of this book and the READ3 Model like a counseling program for both American individuals and America as a whole.

The READ3 Model describes the steps involved in making productive moves forward in our lives—both individually and collectively. It makes the point that reading, quite literally, is a unique activity that promotes learning and growth. Representationally, each letter stands for a critical moment in the developmental process:

R stands for Revelation, the "aha" beginning of new learning.

E stands for Exploration, where we push deeper to understand the nuances and applications of our new understanding.

A stands for Action, since it is only through putting these new understandings into action and testing them out through experience that they take root and gain meaning. And service action in particular is critical to growth. The act of serving others has a unique way of opening our minds and hearts to new awareness.

D3 stands for the triple tasks of Discovery—stopping to understand what you've learned from action; Dreaming—letting those discoveries, good or bad, lead to a compelling picture of the future; and Declarations of Interdependence—actually writing down the things that you intend and by which you will be guided.

Chapter 3

The Developmental Insight: A Teenage Nation and Growth with the Years

Let's talk first about what's happening in our country now that we've entered the phase of late adolescence. It's important to understand that the following processes occur whether or not we grab hold of the growth wheel.

Developmental psychology tells us that with the passing of years, every single human—and perhaps every nation—goes through predictable patterns in aging. The kind of growth that happens with years is called *maturational development*. We see it in nature around us as a core to all of life.

Maturational development marks the age-related phases and tasks that correlate with normal brain and body developments.[20] It's the something that we may try hard to override but, in the end, really cannot.

These phases are well documented and intrinsic to the human condition: sight and cognition in infancy, learning trust vs. mistrust in toddler years, childhood formations of feelings and worldviews, the egocentric nature of adolescence, and the questions of generativity or stagnation we face in full maturity.

It seems self-evident that a nation has similar collective patterns that echo the human ones. We can see the United

States as developmentally analogous to a newborn, toddler, child, preteen, and adolescent.

The human adolescent can't skip this developmental phase, and neither can the country.

We can't deny or go around it.

We must go through it.

Understanding these maturational parallels can bring insight into our present collective conditions and unavoidable needs. The human adolescent can't skip this developmental phase, and neither can the country. We can't deny or go around it. We must go through it.

There are many parallels between the present United States as a developmental adolescent and our understanding of adolescence as a stage.

Teens are egocentric, meaning their world is self-referential. The story is *always* about them. The response is always about them. Someone tells a story, and the teen responds with something in their own experience that is the same or with "That's never happened to me."

They can't help it. Their understanding of the world starts with an understanding of self, so it naturally follows that the whole world is seen only in the ways it interacts directly with them.

Teens: The story is *always* about them. The response is always about them. They can't help it. Isn't that the way of the US today?

It's hard for a teen to give good counsel to others because they can only see their own experience: "Here's what I did when that happened to me." Or "I've never had anyone do that to me." Or "What I'd do if that were me…"

We struggle with this very phenomenon as a nation today. It's hard to appreciate cultural differences because, as a whole, we are seeing only our experiences. Empathy and perspective-taking are relatively rare capabilities.

Here are some of the ways that we as a nation exhibit the characteristics of a late-stage teen—a mixed bag of the good, the bad, and the ugly, depending on how it manifests and is used:

- Egocentrism
  - The world is built around me
  - If it's not about me, I'm not really interested; I'm mostly working on me
  - Belief that everyone is looking at me
  - Interest in self-reflection
- Cliquish behavior
  - Exaltation of "friends" and group identity
  - Need for affirmations from the group that I'm okay

- Looking for group affiliations and outer declarations (clothing, language, etc.)
- Identity crisis
  - Mirror fascination (studying "me" in every type of mirror I find)
  - Name and family identity
  - Who am I? (a repeated theme with variations in poetry, prose, and song)
  - The belief that self-expression is more important than practically anything else
- Brief attention span
  - Entertainment-focused, pleasure-seeking
  - Short views, shortened phrases and messages
- Immortality (little sense of personal consequences for today's actions)
- Fiscally unaware (the money is sort of magic… it just comes)
- Physically irresponsible (risking life and injury)
- Loud and bold
- Fascination with sex
- Highly emotional
- Angry, anxious, offended
- Loving, devoted, passionate
- More interesting than interested

All of these characteristics—markers of the classic late-stage teenager—seem to shout from the day's headlines and social-media feeds. The ascendancy of the tweet is one of dozens of examples that represent many of these impulses at work: our short attention spans, focus on entertainment, interest in garnering a "win" in the form of social support, and our fascination with selfies and egocentrism.

This might not seem like good news, which is the best news of all. If the list of teenage attributes strikes us as undesirable, then we're already seeing through a more mature lens. And when we can start to see something, we can start to change it. Just as the final years in high school were full of opportunity and important decisions, the immediate years ahead are that for us.

As we move into the 2020s, we are moving from our sophomore year in high school toward graduation and thoughts of the future. At our core, we really do want to become something, to dream of a great future, and to believe that there are good things ahead for us. The wonderful part of being in late adolescence as a country is that we have an unlimited supply of passion, idealism, and confidence in our abilities to work it all out. We want hope. All things are built around hope. And we're finding it.

We're changing in some important ways right now. In 2016, the Pew Report documented the first-ever reversal in the popularity of living with parents vs. partners. Their published report devoted much space to why this reversal has happened. They opined many possibilities common to the national dialogue, but they neglected one of the most intriguing psychological factors: developmental psychology.

We want hope. All things are built around hope. And we're finding it.

Late-stage teens secure their support base before launching into new vistas. We often see a renewed closeness in the family toward the high school graduation, for instance. Parents and teens frequently get closer during this time, savoring some special moments before the next maturational move begins. And we're likely to see this kind of trend continue on a larger scale in the United States for a few years as we make our way through this maturational stage as a country. That means that families will seem closer right now, spend more time in each other's company, count each other as friends, and have an expectation that parents and children should be arm-linked—or at least phone-linked—as we move through this stage of our country's growth.

In 2019, more adult children lived with their parents than at any point in history. And among those adult children with partners and children of their own, the majority also vacationed (where vacations were accessible) with their parents. This was true across all socioeconomic groups.

In 1960, 72 percent of American adults ages eighteen and older were married. Today, just over half are. In 2013, about three-quarters of adults said their relationships with their adult children were mostly positive and only two percent said they were mostly negative. Most interestingly, parents frequently mentioned a relationship with a grown child as a source of enjoyment in their lives—86 percent of them considered their relationships with their children this way.[21]

One could draw from this information that parents and children are working on interdependence. Logically, if the living-at-home dynamic were about sustained dependence—or even independence—parents would be unlikely to report their relationships with grown children as a source of enjoyment, as they overwhelmingly do. For most of us, reporting that a relationship is a source of enjoyment means that it goes both ways, with care for all involved.

The path to good familial relationships begins as new adolescents first evaluate their parents' marriages. In order to forge their own romantic relationships, teens begin by looking at the closest relationships that they can examine and understand. Next, they try out relationships, at first in an independent way, in the quest for identity and a sense of completion or fulfillment. And finally, late adolescents recognize that relationships are about each other, about what you are together.

Whereas early adolescents exhibit "get away from the parents" behavior, more mature adolescents pull back toward their parents before "launching" into more distinct adult relationships.

On a national level, we are seeing these late-adolescent dynamics played out (not by adolescents but by all of American society). This moment in America is such a land of opportunity.

Early adolescents typically display a fascination with all things sexual. Everything is giggling innuendo or a glimpse of flesh. Late adolescents, on the other hand, begin to integrate sexual drives with ideas of love and connection. And while early adolescents are egocentric and self-reinforcing with their social groups, later adolescents add nuanced questions of identity and becoming.

Late adolescence is a period of examining the parental relationship in careful ways, and this stage is where, most often, criticisms of the parents' relationship are born. These criticisms are born of hopes for a different sort of future and, at least some of the time, a uniform set of notions about what relationships are.

On a national level, we are seeing these late-adolescent dynamics played out. We are looking at our democratic "parent" system in careful ways, and we have much criticism for that system today. These criticisms are born of hopes for a different, improved sort of future. And it is likely that, at least some of the time, they are also the product of an uninformed notion of what the democratic system, with its interdependent relationships, really is. If we believe that the relationship between governmental systems (the "parents" in America's world) is dysfunctional and flawed, then we will surely seek something different for our future. If we believe that there are good relationships among the branches of government and party systems, then we will likely support and shape our future around those core ideals.

Like those last moments of high school, this moment in America is such a land of opportunity. And the thing we tell our children is a message for ourselves:

you're going to live with today's decisions for a long while. Choose carefully, because it will shift the trajectory of the next few decades.

We can trace the move to late adolescence as a country in the pattern of the evolution of US media over the last few decades, where we have moved from a fascination with all things sexual to an interest in relationships and love. (Here again we see the echoes of the rootedness young adults are displaying today as they linger and form more familial relationships around chosen core values.)

As a nation, we no longer get the thirteen-year-old giggles when we hear a reference to genitals. Like an older sister dealing with a younger sibling, our reaction is more annoyance than titillation. Our adolescent nation remains fascinated with sexuality, but our interest has taken a turn toward the deeper psychological dynamics behind it: identity, love, and values.

Looking at entertainment as a barometer of national interest and developmental shifts, we find ample evidence that we have moved through the stages of teenage development in the past fifty years. In our TV shows, we see the evolving treatment of sexuality, as well as parental relationships that track closely to our national life stages, from early adolescence to our current late adolescence/young adult stage. Let's take a little closer of a look at our national views as reflected from our home screens.

America's Early Adolescence: 1960s–1990s

In the '50s and early '60s, human sexuality was on America's mind, but like a new teen, we studiously avoided all reference to it in our entertainment. We stuck to our *Gunsmoke* and *Green Acres* and clung to Mayberry, where Andy made us all feel more comfortable about the changes through which we were moving. Sexuality was relegated to fringe conversations, hidden *Playboy* magazines, and emergent illicit porn. Parents engendered respect— as in *Father Knows Best* and *My Three Sons*—and although they were sometimes humorous and misinformed, in the end, the parent always *did* know more than the kids.

For those who have seen the iconic *Leave It to Beaver* from the 1950s, the moral of the story could be that young Beaver or his brother Wally had a good point or different view, but parents Mr. and Mrs. Cleaver were going to pull it all together with the right perspective. Early adolescents have not really seen their parents as people yet. Parents in these shows were most often mystery boxes with no real backstories. What do we know of the motherly character June Cleaver other than her pearls, apron, and perpetually concerned expression?

In the '70s, our adolescent nation's fascination with sexuality and the explorations of the late '60s inched into the social mainstream dialogue and onto our small screens at home. Americans giggled at Fonzie's sexual innuendo, as even "Ayyyyyy…" seemed racy in *Happy*

American Society's Teen Years Reflected in our Entertainment

Going through our collective teen years with *Friends*, we learned about sex, love, and relationships.

Days. *M*A*S*H*'s nickname for "Hot Lips Houlihan" was one of dozens of examples of boundary-pushing as we edged into some of our first beyond-the-birds-and-bees public conversations about sex as a country.

Archie Bunker brilliantly introduced social studies for our American context from his famous lounge chair in the groundbreaking *All in the Family*, taking the iconic place of a parent from a developmental thirteen-year-old's perspective: gruff, out of touch, and unrelatable.

Our nation was pretty much a big thirteen-year-old when *All in the Family* debuted in January of 1971. Edith and

Archie were painted as a nonsexual, non-relational couple. Archie's interest was in his TV and iconic chair, from which he rarely moved. Edith served all and was seen only with a sideways glance by Archie. Through the younger people on the show, there was an introduction to different points of view. The brilliance of the show's writing permitted our nation, the early adolescents that we were, to push against these parental archetypes and denounce their belief systems. In one of the first episodes, Mike, Edith and Archie's live-in son-in-law, writes a letter to President Nixon protesting everything that's wrong with America, including the state of the environment and the nation's involvement in Vietnam. Archie finds out, and to refute his son-in-law's claims, he decides he also will write a letter, praising the nation's chief. Throughout the show's nine-season run, themes of women's equality and racial bias were regularly addressed, painting Archie as a questionable "sage" at best and the embodiment of America's phobias at worst.

Another show known for its edgy racial humor, running gags, and catchphrases also featured the younger generation as wiser and more levelheaded with a cantankerous and contentious father. This series arrived on the screen a year after the Bunker Family and offered the imagined perspective of a Black family. *Sanford and Son* painted the peaceful, longsuffering, conscientious, and progressive son, Lamont, in juxtaposition with the attention-seeking and closed-minded father, Fred. America seemed to be working out

a couple of things in this series. Perhaps tellingly, I didn't learn until researching for this book that this show was viewed by many as a misrepresentation of Black lives in America and as misinformation. Through today's lens, that assessment makes sense. It may reinforce the fact that our adolescent nation was, in this perhaps skewed representation of Black culture, continuing to present an unrelatable "adult" alongside a wise "adult child" in another way.

The 1970s American dialogue was maturing from the stick-figure characterizations of both literal and figurative black-and-white TV that presented parents as wise but distant archetypes to color-filled versions of parents seen through a radically different teenage lens. We moved from *Father Knows Best* toward "What does Father really know?" We laughed at the father figures and shook our heads at their outdated ways, feeling proud of our more modern perspectives.

In the 1980s and early 1990s, our country found its way into middle adolescence, the hallowed ground of high school freshmen and sophomores. More contemplative shows like *Frasier* and *Seinfeld* became the mainstays of primetime TV, reflecting our desire to laugh but also to think deeply. By now, sex talk was out and out—and funny—as the previously forbidden became fodder for family-room laughs.

Sex took center stage, as though we were engaged in a national group class on human sexuality. As we made *Friends*, we began to chart the path from the giggling pre-adolescent obsessed with glimpses of porn to the middle teen occupied by deeper relationships and future-looking concerns.

Parents were still a fringe element and rarely explored in anything beyond a cardboard placeholder. Do you know anything about Monica and Ross's (*Friends*) parents other than that they were funny and seemingly preferred Ross? The emphasis was on the peer group, the egocentric personal experience.

Friends gave us a view into a variety of aspects of relationships within that peer perspective. We explored Ross with his child, his ex-wife, and her partner, as well as Joey and Chandler's relationship as roommates, the female peers navigating each other and their sometimes overlapping or conflicting romantic relationships, and the varied individual relationships of each cast member. Part of the show's continuing appeal is that it took multiple perspectives and played them out. Conservative or Liberal or unsure, you thought that show was for you.

The idea of presenting multiple perspectives was totally fresh—and refreshing—and we saw it play out in other relationship-oriented shows built around the peer group. Shows like *Golden Girls*, *Seinfeld*, *Frasier*, *The Fresh Prince of Bel-Air*, and *Living Single* gave us peer groups where we explored relationships and intimacy in myriad different ways. And though sex remained a humorous, even central, theme in all of the shows, it wasn't really about sexuality. It was about understanding how to be in a relationship with someone who was (just a little) different than you.

Developmentally, we know that, inside, we retain our five-year-old selves alongside our fifteen-year-old selves. One way of thinking is that we are—always—not only our biological age but also all the ages that have come before. *Golden Girls* illustrated with ripe humor that we are indeed all the ages we've ever been, as the show featured people who were parents and grandparents as *people*, with the same peer interests as those much younger. It was remarkable to start to think about parents and grandparents not as folks sitting around waiting to make cookies for the littles. They were people with roaring sex drives, childish pet peeves, and a young adult's interest in new things. They had priorities of their own with activities that wouldn't make the cut for a G-rated "Greatest Grandma" life reel.

Seinfeld gave us one of the first glimpses of parents as people through the eyes of their children. (Who could forget the Costanzas?) While the children saw their parents only peripherally, they were loved and respected, even when they failed to understand their parents' ways.

Frasier gave us parents as people, too, revising the uninformed Archie Bunker father figure of the '70s to a father personality that had a different sort of life experience and personal wisdom. Less educated, fussy, and eloquent than his son, he was nonetheless full of admirable qualities and intent, with a centering sort of influence. The show gave room to let the father move from stick figure to "Dad" personhood.

Living Single even blended reality and fiction by including the real-life moms of two of the principles playing their mothers in an early episode. In a show focused on six friends in a Brooklyn brownstone and their peer and professional dynamics, this nod to reality was one of the ways we were taking down a glass wall between adult children and their parents in America.

America's Move Through High School: Late Adolescence: 2000–Present

Twenty-first-century TV and streaming shows have reflected the shift into the later teen years for our country in alignment with the simultaneous emergence of the first generation that reports wanting to spend extended time with their parents and families.

In the individual adolescent, we remember that it is a milestone (just like walking or talking) for a young person to form an opinion about their parents' relationship. The child has developed enough to see her parents as fallible, as people. From there, the child can begin to evaluate the parents and their relationship in order to create a model for herself. Do I want that type of relationship? What do I believe is accurate or right about my parents' relationship? What do I believe is wrong? This makes parents decidedly uncomfortable—no one wants to be judged or criticized. And the child doesn't really understand what she's seeing either.

At thirteen, we are almost ready to view our parents as people, full of quirks and foibles as well as unique strengths. This helps us stand apart and evaluate them without censure. It's a part of learning. If a child can have a rational opinion about his or her parents' relationship, that child has given evidence of moving through a developmental stage.

Ask thirteen-year-olds James and Joaquin about their parents' relationships, and you might get answers like this: "My parents are cool. They really love me," or "My parents are really strict." (Notice how in both cases, the response is about the child's experience, not about the parents.)

But ask sixteen-year-old Judith the same question, and the answer is likely to be very different: "I don't want to have a relationship like my parents'. They never even touch. I'm not sure they actually love one another."

Or seventeen-year-old Cheryl: "My parents have been fighting about the same basic things for as long as I can remember. I hate to watch them go through that and hope I never have that in my relationship."

Ding, ding, ding, ding!

Our national views in the 1960s were a lot like those of a developmental thirteen-year-old. On TV, parents were not "real" but figurative: June Cleaver's apron and concerned eyebrow raise.

The sixteen-year-old's perspective looks a lot more like our TV perspectives in the 1970s: parents were often flawed, and those flaws were something we pushed against in order to form revised worldviews. In the 1980s and '90s, parents were separate people from peer groups, where the "real" relationships formed.

Try This: Your Turn—Take Stock of the Things You Observe

Are you a list-maker?

No? You may want to move on, as this idea is for the list-makers among us, and there will be other ideas for you.

Yes? Then this will make your day! Here are a couple of lists for your contemplation:

1. List people you know over the age of eighteen who live with their parent or parents.

2. List fifteen adults you know. How many of them see or spend time with their immediate family regularly?

3. List the top fifteen news stories right now and categorize them:
    i.   Facts and information of import to society
    ii. Entertainment
    iii. Political sensationalism (including outrage, upset, etc.) repeating an established theme—insignificant new information
    iv. Actionable information for you

From these lists, what do you see? Do you see our nation's adolescent dynamics in evidence?

Between 2000 and 2020, we've witnessed the final stage of adolescence. On television, we've begun to see parents as full people that are part of the children's lives.

From silly frolics like *Modern Family* to *How I Met Your Mother*, we explored the dynamics of adulting (and we even coined the word) in new ways. More recently, in comedies like *Schitt's Creek*, we've seen depictions of parents and children as partners—flawed to exaggerated effect but lovable, and facing life's challenges with skill, even if there are some mess-ups. The lingering connection between children and their parents into traditional adulthood that the show

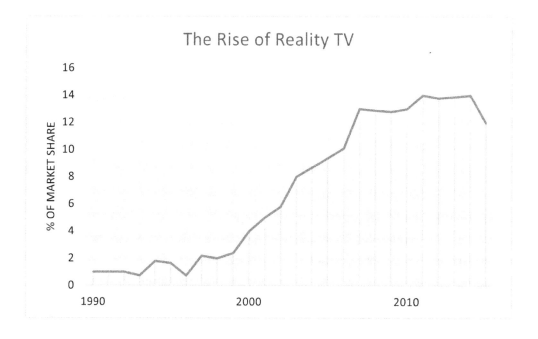

The Rise of Reality TV

depicts, if not quite normalized, is not viewed as dysfunctional, either.

This move toward more balanced familial views is paralleled by the rise of unscripted entertainment in America's "late teen" years. Culturally, our late-teen perspectives have been reflected in the rise of reality TV as we have explored intimacy and relationships in whole new ways. Like a real-life version of *Friends* or *Frasier*, reality TV has given us an unscripted version of peer relationship exploration. As odd as reality TV (and reality) looks, I believe it reflects part of our growing up as a country.

On the scripted side of the early twenty-first century, we saw life get messy and take on more dramatic depth. From *Grey's Anatomy* to *Desperate Housewives* to *Mad Men* to *Two and a Half Men*, TV reflected our desire to see life's struggles from various perspectives.

But perhaps no TV show more defines and delaminates our current era than *Keeping Up with the Kardashians*, which, unlike the previously mentioned programs, is unscripted. While this show has been critically panned by many and is a guilty pleasure to others, we cannot escape the fact that our society has been keeping up with the Kim, Kris, Kourtney, and Khloé since 2007. As frivolous as it seems, the Kardashians captivated the attention of so many because the show pulled us into a voyeuristic reality that blends real life with entertainment. I've never watched the show, and yet I still know that Kim Kardashian got a new yellow bikini this summer and that Caitlyn Jenner has transitioned. I know about the Kardashians. They have a hold on our culture.

I would argue that reality TV led the way for one of the most profound cultural shifts of the last two decades: the rise of social media. Social media is its own kind of reality TV, and the star is me. And you. And us.

Can you even remember the world before Facebook? Smartphones? iPhones? Instagram? LinkedIn? Twitter? Snapchat? Marco Polo? The list is getting longer every day.

The world before Facebook had a much stronger delineation between private and public. People called a home phone line. Callers' numbers didn't appear automatically on a screen to identify them; people chose whether to leave their numbers on your message machine at the beep. Photos were shared at family gatherings and kept in photo albums on shelves or under a bed. If you wanted to make a video, you needed to lug out a big camera or hire a professional videographer.

Now, we are all writers, photographers, and video-production houses with an electronic device or two for our family, business, and dear-diary moments. If we want to capture a thought now, we feel the need to put it out there. The average American watches eight to ten videos online every day.[22] And in 2020, Allison Sadlier of the *New York Post* published a study of 2,000 Americans with access to streaming content and related that the average person was watching eight hours per day.[23]

Try This: Seeing Your Parents as People (Not as Parents)

Developmentally, teens must recognize their parents as people in a relationship that is separate from themselves before having their own adult relationships. In this way, the teen moves farther away from the "I create everything" centrality of childhood and the "Everything revolves around me" centrality of adolescence. By seeing a parental relationship as separate from ourselves and then forming a perspective about that relationship (noting the dynamics, the patterns, and the shifts), we adolescents prepare ourselves to form our own desires for relationships, with values and opinions about the kinds of things we desire to have in our lives.

Experience:

In a discussion with others, present your parents as people, with no reference to how they are with you as a child. Describe their lives, choices, work, beliefs, and loves as individuals. Avoid "They _____ me" sentences and keep your dialogue about them. Ask questions of each other. Imagine you are creating characters for a movie.

Over the past twenty years, we have become the most documented culture and species ever to roam the planet. But isn't that what young people in their late adolescence do? They write culminating senior letters; they take pictures and make floats and try to remember Every. Single. Moment. (With varying motives and drivers.)

We have framed our own reality shows. We write the scripts and invite our audience. We may seek intimate audiences or cast a broad net. Either way, our personal realities and our entertainment have blurred.

Almost every popular television show today explores, in one way or another, our own reality in some psychological depth. Shows like *The Good Fight* and *Designated Survivor* and *House of Cards* have blended current events with fictitious characters, exploring our present dilemmas in ways that were at first barely veiled and then out-and-out blunt. And the Kardashians have ended their "show," but worry not. They're just embracing the next level of reality: relationships with their viewers through emergent media trends. Now they're like old friends their fans interact with daily through media. In 2020, Kim Kardashian's Instagram following was more than double the number of votes of any elected official—a testimony to our we-are-the-entertainment and we-are-the-news current state.

What does that have to do with our maturation as a country? Ah! That's the incredibly cool part.

Using the language of late-adolescent development, we are doing some deep explorations into trying to figure out who we are.

We're like a bunch of seventeen- and eighteen-year-olds trying to figure out our identity, trying to understand our passions, trying to sort through our faith and figure out who and what we want to be going forward. People don't take endless pictures of themselves because they have forgotten—or are celebrating—the way they look. They're trying to see themselves.

We're trying to see ourselves. We're trying to find a mirror, and it's not about being the fairest of all, but about being.

Without a witness, it is hard for a late-stage teen to believe they even exist. Sports give a frame and meaning to their activities. Celebrations, parties, and rituals are all about saying, "Here you are."

So, America, here we are. We are here. We are crossing the stage from our adolescent high school years into those young-adult spaces. And it is changing everything.

Adulting America

The parent-child hierarchy has given way today to a relationship that is closer and more intimate than has ever existed in US history. It's a national thing. During the COVID-19 crisis, videos of families dancing together, playing together, or making something humorous circulated on the internet with wonderful frequency. It has become commonplace to see parents and children protesting together for passionate social causes, taking on entrepreneurship adventures together, or inventing something as a family.

On a national scale, America's media reflects this developmental movement, as all generations have started to come together into one striated culture. Our Netflix and TV shows no longer feature those background parent figures pulling the strings or influencing children's decisions from behind the scenes. (We even have shows, like the wildly popular *Grace and Frankie*, that center the parent figures.) Everyone has become just…

people. It can actually make watching a series mentally challenging, these days! Everyone has a backstory, a full story, a life line to follow. Binge-watching is about grabbing those really big books and getting into all of the characters.

The onset of the novel coronavirus pandemic only seemed to take these trends farther. America expanded from reality TV shows and reality postings from friends to reality Zooms streaming alongside our interests. Unscripted life moved from a production set into people's homes—an intimate move involving casual dress and a glimpse of people in their natural habitats and with their natural hair. Something changes when people take off their shoes and have a conversation from their kitchens.

But even as we require less fanfare than ever before, something is shifting with regard to our short attention spans. For about a decade, I edited commercial and familial videos as an artistic passion on the side of my other work. My edits tended to change the image every two to four seconds, which marked them as "para-professional" work, because in commercial editing, the images were changed every second or less. This reflects our ability to absorb a lot of media quickly and our adolescent impatience to go fast and high in our entertainment. It would appear we've come through this media phase where things must shift multiple times a second and returned to prolonged attention spans where we want more depth or more reality. In the 2020s, talking heads are often presented with a single unchanging shot. This type of watching has become normalized. And according to a 2019 study published in *The New York Times* by Jaclyn Peiser,[24] more than half the people in the United States "have listened to one [podcast], and nearly one out of three people listen to at least one podcast every month." Is this caused by distrust of the editing process, since we know it can distort meaning, or is it a different sort of maturity feeding this trend?

This is reason to take heart as we take on the task of adulting America. We're trying to decide what we know, and that quest has led us into deeper dives on the subjects that concern and interest us. Instead of a highly edited two-minute brief, we're interested in a forty-five-minute podcast interview that is, or feels, unedited.

Doesn't this seem like a gravitation back to our great grandparents' hearths and family radio, with a 2020s twist?

On the one hand, we must acknowledge that our attention span remains miniscule, communicating via limited characters and letters. And on the other, we've learned to get into a big story, delve deeply into a podcast series or even a team video game, and stay there.

And like that of a late adolescent moving into adulthood, the quest for America's identity shifts from "Who am I?" to "Who do I want to be?"

A late adolescent/early young adult contemplates work contributions, longterm relationships, keeping or changing names, chosen community, and expressing an identity that is both new and rooted in something valuable from the

Music Matters

Another example of our past and current developmental state as a country is in our music. In most mature cultures throughout all of time, music genres have been shared. A whole family appreciated the same artists and songs, danced the same dances, and experienced music together, regardless of age or generation.

In the 1960s, during America's move into full adolescence, our developmental journey was clearly reflected in musical separations and rifts. The iconic Woodstock references a musical revolution that represented not only America's increasing sense of separate identities, but also questioning authority, exploring ideas and possibilities beyond what was offered by parents, and determining our own paths.

Before the 1960s, the family radio offered one genre of music and dancing, and other forms of enjoyment were shared. But in the 1960s and continuing into the '70s and '80s, "the music of youth" had clear voices that were differentiated from those of adults. It is not normal for a culture to be divided in its music. And that early-adolescent separation has taken about fifty years to return to the world norm of sharing a musical culture.

As we move through adolescence into our young adulthoods, we're coming back together musically. Families share playlists, concert tickets, festivals, and Amazon's Alexa in the twenty-first century. Through musical exploration fueled by access to various channels (from radio to streaming to YouTube to Apple Music to others), music is again one of the biggest connecting pieces of familial culture.

past. The United States today is facing those same extended questions of identity: What does my heritage mean? What

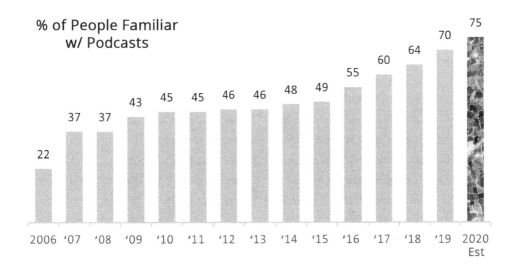

% of People Familiar w/ Podcasts

does my culture mean? Will I keep this name? What images do we want to represent us? I value democracy and the name America—how do I reconcile the parts we cherish and the parts we want to change going forward?

It is common to paint all of this as an impossible crisis, but I want us to try a different frame. The developmental frame says that the questions we're addressing today follow the pattern we've been in for the past 240 years and reflect a very normal trajectory of human development. If the past tells us anything about where we're going now as a country, it says that this is indeed a moment of great opportunity for us. This is the moment we choose who we want to be and what we want to do for the next 240 years.

And the great news is that we seem to be listening to others, looking more deeply for answers, and taking this more seriously than at any point since the American Revolution.

In twenty-first-century America, our entertainment has fragmented from a shared conversation to hundreds of divergent interests and extreme explorations of questions of faith, love, violence, history, sexuality, and identity. And while, in certain quarters, we are experiencing a bit of a panic attack over what may seem like national chaos, let me play school counselor for a second and assure all of us that this behavior is normal for a teen.

At the risk of being repetitive, the trick to getting through adolescence is staying alive. We've done that—yay! Now, our next step is getting through this spot in our country's development. We'll do the work individually. That's the only way growth happens. But an awareness that we're part of a collective development is a helpful perspective: it helps us understand that we're working toward a better, stabler, safer, and more satisfying society together. At some level of our collective intuition, we are aware of the shift. When the pandemic created the national sequestering, the first response was a reassuring "We're in this together… together… together" in practically every ad and offering. Knowing that we're all on the same trajectory as a country is a powerful thing.

We're trying to make decisions about our future as a young-adult nation that won't destroy our planet or burn bridges with the rest of the world. But we're good nearly adult kids, essentially: diverse, interested kids with an emergent "generation citizen." This new generation feels compelled to be active and involved in shaping their citizenship and communities. There is even an organization called Generation Citizen that has as its vision "a country of young people working as active and effective citizens to collectively strengthen our American democracy."[25]

In the 2020s, our entertainment reflects connected familial relationships and acknowledges and explores parental sexuality, conflict, collaboration, sacrificial love, and more. These trends are representative of our reality. We accept sexuality as a normal part of the cultural dialogue, but it is no longer the titillating focus. Instead, identity and future concerns have taken center stage in our late-adolescent dialogue.

The Pew Research Center reports that more than half of eighteen-to-twenty-nine-year-olds have contact with their parents every day. The same report validates the statistic in the other direction: the majority of both mothers and fathers report having daily contact with their adult children almost every day, if not every day. This is not only a shift in familial contact, but a shift in traditional parental roles. Just a decade or so ago, "Call your mother" might have been a stereotypical joke.

Today, it would likely fall flat, as the majority of children are calling both their mother and their father over the course of daily activity. In a separate study, scholars Karen Fingerman and Frank Furstenberg underscore how different today's rate of connecting is from the past: In 1986, about half of parents reported that they had spoken with a grown child in the past week. In 2008, 87 percent said they had. In 1988, less than half of parents had given advice to a grown child in the past month, and fewer than one in three had provided any hands-on help. Recent data show that nearly 90 percent of parents now give advice and 70 percent provide some type of practical assistance.[26]

We're seeing new levels of self-reported positive feelings between the generations, grounded in the intimacy that comes from frequent interactions and knowledge of the little ups and downs of everyday life.

The way through this developmental journey is *through* it—and transitions in development to the next phases can be facilitated by intent or received with surprise. That's the choice in front of us today as a country.

What are we becoming?

What do we want to become?

According to Bella DePaulo, PhD, our newfound closeness "is not simply a side

Try This: Experience All That Third Spaces Facilitate

Retailers that extend stories and introduce new ideas, like independent bookstores and museum stores, are in vogue. Also "in" are "third spaces," which provide an experience in addition to or in the place of consumption, because experiences are what we need to facilitate our becoming. We are interested in action.

Today, experience is the thing we are seeking, and we find it—along with the other people with whom we need to develop our interdependent thinking—in these spaces.

Look for them in your area. Chances are, you have at least a few—an independent bookstore, a library, a social area or hangout at a church, a coffee shop, a game space, a green space, or a park.

And in those third spaces, try looking up and around at what and whom you notice. Heighten your awareness of the dynamics around you. Like an anthropologist, throw yourself into an interesting study and experience the world around you—with others.

effect of a bad economy or the ubiquity of cellphones." It is about the hug from friends or family—that moment we pull it all in as we contemplate what comes next.[27]

Collectively, we are pulling in closely as families for those warm hugs as we contemplate who we will become as a country. The emergent trend of family board games reported through the American Booksellers Association reflects our late adolescence as a nation as we seek familial interaction as a path to the formation of our identity. In an era of technology, experiences together—conversation, games, and general time spent in one another's company—have taken on new primacy.[28]

Family—crew, team, group, "us"—we need this as a foundation for our identity quest. And adult identity is the quest of the hour for our nation.

Like a nation of tenth-grade poets, we have been a chorus of "Who am I?" contemplations. We have pulled close to "our people"—whoever they may be—where we have found an invested and interested audience for our musings.

Growth is messy, and some of us are still in those musings, filling blogs and pushing in and with and against each other with a near-insatiable appetite for more musings, pictures, and videos. This is all part of the path toward adulthood.

Perhaps more than any other country on its developmental journey, we are struggling with things like personal pronouns and monikers. Though there is plenty of persecution in the outer world, in our intimate communities, we have found safe spaces for connection and development, contemplation and prayer. We are a nation of people looking for acceptance. Over and over, we see people asking the question "Am I okay?" The answer writ large in our entertainment is generally, "Yes, tell me more."

Human development is an integrative science. It stands back and says, "This is what we can observe." But it also offers solutions and interventions to help individuals move forward and avoid becoming stuck. While some of our growth is maturational—and comes whether we invite it or not with the passage of years—there is also growth that is chosen. We want to do more than survive these last adolescent years: we want to thrive. This is where we now turn our attention, with chosen development and the READ3 Model.

Chapter 4

Toward Interdependence:
The Growth We Choose in READ3

I F YOU RECALL from the opening pages, I mentioned we're tracing two different kinds of development in this book. The first is that automatic, unavoidable kind that comes with time: maturational development. As long as we survive, we'll undergo certain changes. I've chosen to focus first on this type of development because it forms the scaffolding of the analogy. When we can make the leap up 5,000 feet to see our whole country on a time-centered maturational path, we've got some traction to understand this spot in our country's life. Understanding where we are, where we've been, and where we're immediately headed in maturational terms is a really useful thing.

We can see this moment as one of the most hopeful in our nation's history.

The second kind of development comes when we make the difficult choice to grow. This is called hierarchical development. I will also refer to it as "chosen development," since, unlike maturational development, it's not a given part of getting older, but rather something we must exercise conscious effort toward achieving. Chosen development is really where the developmental toolkit comes in. Since you've read this far, chances are pretty strong that you are interested in growth. Perhaps you are among the estimated 25% of our country already capable of abstraction and perspective-taking, or perhaps you recognize yourself, as I did, as among the 75% who did not possess that capability.[29] When, in the course of my developmental psychology studies, I learned that there was more development to be had—that my ways of thinking and processing could be enhanced with learning—I was excited. I hope you meet this awareness with hope, inspiration, and encouragement. For all of us, there is more!

As I write this chapter, we're in the midst of the COVID-19 pandemic. The global crisis has become a national one of a political sort, with ugly battles about masks raging in many places in the country as people sort out what safety and social responsibility mean.

We are awaiting an attempt at justice for the brutal murder of Ahmaud Arbery in Georgia.[30] We have watched the video footage of George Floyd's death and other incomprehensible acts that seem to violate what we believe it means to be thinking, loving humans.[31] It is an odd time to speak of hope. But this book is about hope in some monumental ways.

Our hope depends not on our gifts of intelligence or the information we get, but on how we process that information. There are many types of intelligences—emotional, physical, intellectual, spiritual—and all play a role in the pursuit of chosen development.

Just as we don't expect a toddler to understand the consequences of death or social injustice and we don't expect a ten-year-old to be capable of running a business, we need to recognize that we as a nation have collective limitations on our ability to perceive, process, and make decisions.

While we have much to learn about hierarchical development, we are in the midst of a must-do-now moment of maturational development that is happening with or without our deliberate participation. Thirty years from now, the era in which these pages were written will mark a turning point in our country: that time when we were collectively on the cusp of becoming an adult nation. I hope we look back with feelings of pride and gratitude about the choices we made in the second decade of the twenty-first century. And I hope we also see this as a time when more people grabbed the wheel of their own development and took themselves for a drive.

Like a twentysomething Ben Franklin, it's time we choose the virtues by which we want to live our lives. It's time to determine where we will put our faith and what things matter most. This is the space in which we will define the cadence and nature of our society going forward, what we want our neighborhoods to look like, and what we want to do and be together in the global world of work and play.

Let's think about the various important talks that we expect to have with individual late adolescents. Think about a child of eighteen and the kinds of conversations a caring parent initiates. There's the faith talk, the sex talk, the relationship talk, the career talk, the health talk, the family talk, the contribute-to-society talk, the money talk. How might we have those talks from a national maturational perspective?

Let's consider the topics our nearly adulting nation needs to consider and start with the one that makes us squirm most: money.

Chapter 5

Money, News, and How We Decide What We Know

Money and Maturation for All of Us

IT'S HARD FOR a teen to perceive that everything he does, everything he is surrounded by, came from some sort of resource that was almost always bartered for money. He has the keys to the car, the keys to the house, and a card for food. How those things get funded is sort of a magical mystery. Parents funding these magical mystery tours are hard-pressed to get the message across that money is finite and acquired with difficulty.

Let's consider a hypothetical college student we'll call Carolyn. Carolyn is an idealist who wants to work in radio. She desires a career connecting people with good music, bringing light and life and insights to their worlds. As a senior in college, she lives in a nice home with a big bedroom and has access to all sorts of technology. She also has a real disdain for the pursuit of money, something she sees as crass and greedy. This highly intelligent young woman has gotten almost all A's in her college classes but is no closer to connecting income with life options than she was at three years old. And she has a lot in common with her peers, who are eager to offer something fun and wonderful to the world but unconcerned with how that gets monetized or funded.

It seems the world is divided into those who want to be the wealthiest of all and those who want to work for a nonprofit. The shift toward doing noble work that we love is a reflection of our quest for purpose, toward interdependence, and that's a great thing. But there is a disconnect both for those who imagine immediate and copious wealth and those who dream of great altruistic pursuits. Like the individual adolescent human, our nation struggles to understand the role money plays in all that we pursue.

As an adolescent nation, we've been characterizing money as a lot of rather unreal things: evil, exciting, mysteriously evoked. When we speak of big corporations, we think of piles of magical money shoveled around from yacht to yacht. We watch shows depicting billionaire lifestyles and hear words like "trillions" and "Bitcoin" being thrown around. Money seems like an abstract thing.

In companies large and small, associates can be heard saying, "We'll let the company pay for that," as though there is a magic pot called "company" that births bills on the hour.

A small business is defined as a firm with fewer than 500 employees.[32] Those of us who own one of the 30.7 million small businesses in the US (which account for 99.9 percent of all US businesses) are learning the old lessons of the proverbial lemonade stand bit by bit: money out for resources or raw materials, advertising, and the enterprise itself; money in from sales, which feeds the cycle.

This is where our independence—that adolescent quest with vision and purpose—is missing the wisdom of interdependence needed for true success. It is important to note two statistics available many places (SBA, NFIB, and Fundera) here: 1) only 40% of small businesses are profitable and 2) 82% of businesses fail because of inconsistent or insufficient cash flow.[33]

As I write, the music from the Broadway show *Hamilton* floats through my mind: I don't want to throw away my shot. Like the young Hamilton, we have high aspirations for ourselves and feel the beat of this moment. America seems infused with an entrepreneurial, adolescent spirit as a nation. We're scrappy.[34] And the millennials and Generation Z right behind them have the supreme self-confidence that they cannot fail. So they won't. But they also won't be successful without really coming to terms with this money thing.

According to studies by New York Life Insurance, 65% of millennials will choose self-employment, indicating a steady increase in these small-business numbers.[35] Assuming these numbers are right, we're likely to see more Americans getting a hands-on crash course in how money works. It is hard for even the most educated and intelligent among us to connect the dots between our bank balance, income, and spending decisions.

The small manufacturing company that Dave and I own, Franklin Fixtures, is teeming with talent and intelligence. But cultivating even one individual who understands how money works in the business is difficult. If we need $X per week to pay the payroll, rent, and suppliers, then producing half of that amount in any week is cause for alarm: the deficit is immediate and urgent. The most dedicated employees still view vacation days and time off as a given benefit that's funded mysteriously. We think about those sorts of funds like we used to think about the Tooth Fairy, or perhaps we do not think of them at all but just expect them, like we expect gravity or gas in the pump at the station. But we definitely don't put two and two together.

And the problem of understanding money seems even more pronounced for those who work in institutions and large companies. The highly esteemed professor rarely thinks of how the classroom gets cooled or heated, or how the landscaping outside is done. A top automotive executive might be hard-pressed to state how much she pays in taxes—and which taxes—each pay period, or even the value of the vacations and holidays she receives.

Many years ago, I worked in California in the Los Angeles "southlands" of Manhattan Beach and its surroundings. My job was related to organizational and individual development in the space and defense industry, but I wanted to meet people outside of that realm, so I participated in a book-study group. One of our members graciously opened her home for meetings. Her prebuilt home was in a park that was positioned tightly and noisily under part of Interstate 405 (known locally as "the 405"). She had bars on her windows and cautioned us to arrive and leave before dark. Compelled by her situation, I gingerly asked her about her finances, and she readily explained. She revealed that she paid $750 monthly for the rental of her trailer and $350 monthly for the park-association fees plus utilities (this was in 1991). Remarkably, I had just looked at four different, much better homes on the beach that would cost the same or less. And my gated-community condo with a pool and amenities across from the farmer's market cost less than her trailer. But she didn't know about the choices available to her. She didn't know that she could dine on Rodeo Drive in this cute breakfast place for the same price as McDonald's. She didn't know that my food budget at the farmer's market weekly was half of hers, as she did most of her shopping in a nearby convenience store. We were the same age, skin color, and weight, so I didn't think of my position as one of cultural privilege, but, looking back, it was. I had been exposed to and was aware of choices that she had assumed were out of reach for her budget and her life.

Poverty is a major problem in our country. But the root of that problem isn't only about wages or affordable housing. The root is also about understanding how money works and what choices we have when we spend and invest it.

In our work in manufacturing, Dave and I have made helping our employees understand their resources at work and in our community a priority. There are 430 nonprofits and service organizations in our community, and filtering through them all to find the right one would be a different sort of full-time employment full of frustrating forms and literacy challenges. So now, whenever we meet with our team members individually, we let them know we want to help them in any aspects of their financial, physical, and familial lives where they solicit assistance, and we offer to connect them with services they might not know about. One employee, committed to staying with his ill mother, found it such a relief to know that there were affordable homecare resources that could help him be at work more often and not lose the income. Another employee appreciated knowing his rights for apartment accommodations, given his wife's medical condition. To be clear, this is an offering of a connection rather than an expectation or requirement as part of their employment. We just want to be of help, and employees say they feel empowered by knowing about the resources relevant to their situations. It helps them improve their lives, and that satisfaction is rich for us personally. It is also good for the entire organization and for the team.

While some organizations gain press for installing pool tables and all manner of fun things for employees, we see the knowledge of available services as more fundamental. It may be surprising to learn that there are many intelligent people who do not have a checking account because they feel they cannot manage it or understand how it works. I didn't know why some people ended up living weekly in a motel rather than having an apartment or home before I met people who found themselves in that situation. I didn't understand how some people ended up renting their furniture or in an expensive check-cashing loop. A couple of bad choices, a few unfortunate events, a lack of

understanding about available resources, or good marketing of bad deals can make an individual feel tied up by circumstance. Our goal is to help folks untie those binds and feel confident not only about the money they make in their work, but also how they use it.

This is why money is one of the first things we are talking about as we pursue movement into the next stages of development in America: It is fundamental to our understanding of first independence and then the next achievement, interdependence. Money feels like the most intimate of intimates, so we must work with care and an awareness of this hallowed emotional ground. And interdependence, whether in a small business or a church, means understanding what investing in each other and supporting each other really means.

In the Bible, sixteen of the thirty-eight parables include instructions about money and possessions. In the Gospels, an amazing one out of ten verses (288 in all) deals directly with the subject of money. Perhaps that is because money is a metric not of success but of our development. The way we view, manage, and understand money is first an expression of our understanding of value, appreciation, and gratitude. Then, it is a reflection of our values in action.

When my husband Dave and I invested in Franklin Fixtures five years ago, we didn't realize all that it would require financially from us. There's the story of commitment referencing the chicken and the pig: in the process of making a breakfast of eggs and ham, the chicken is involved, but for the pig, contributing to this meal is an investment of life. It's a frightful thing being all in, and it has stretched both of us in ways we never imagined. But we've learned a lot about how money works, and through that education, we've also learned a lot about ourselves. When we've faced those rock-bottom moments, we've had nothing but our values in front of us: the importance we see in US manufacturing, the quest to build literacy and community, and the opportunity to help thirty-five pretty incredible people work toward their dreams. In other words, our "all in" money is aligned with feelings of purpose and our own continued growth.

As important as it is to talk about money in the world of small-business ownership, where the lessons of money are played out vividly and daily, there remains a reluctance to do so. I realize how quickly and often I tell customers and colleagues that Dave and I take no salary from our manufacturing business, like it's a badge of honor somehow. Reflecting, I ask myself why I do this. I think the answer is that I'm trying to distance myself from the pursuit of money because it feels antithetical to our purpose-driven mission. (Perhaps not unlike my hypothetical college student Carolyn from a few pages ago.) I think my current quest is to make peace with having money—both demystifying it and appreciating it as the critical tool that it is.

If being in business has taught us anything at all, it is that we must understand and manage money. Without healthy bank accounts, nothing moves—no matter how altruistic the aim.

Understanding how society works requires understanding money, sort of like the way understanding how a building holds together requires understanding math. But money is not math.

I once marveled to my friend Jennifer (an industrial engineer by training and birth), "Why is it that the most brilliant mathematicians don't seem to get how money works?" She answered without missing a beat: "Because the two have little to do with each other. Money is about the situations we create and telling stories about how things work so that we can understand what to do. Math is math. They are completely different animals."

While we've embraced the critical advancement of STEM studies in our education system, we've left the proverbial money on the table. Perhaps you are like the many Americans who squirm—just a little—whenever money is mentioned? We've gotten comfortable talking about sex, politics, and religion, but money remains something that few of us discuss with friends, family, or even our children in any depth. In a world where we talk about almost everything with decided and bold irreverence, it continues to feel a little gauche to speak about personal finances.

Why is that? For my part, I suspect we don't talk about money for the same reason that video calls have not completely replaced telephone contact: We don't really feel picture-ready and are vaguely embarrassed at our lack of understanding and control.

In 2010, I was asked to develop a teacher compensation system that used performance-based pay for our local school district. It was to be a national model for teacher pay systems, but immediately, it felt like something was off. The premise was that teachers would be more attentive to results if there were pay dividends associated with their performance. Uncertain that this was an accurate premise, I canvassed the 800-plus teachers in our local schools, asking the question "What is your take-home pay?" Fewer than two percent knew the answer. Educators are not there for the money (a factor that calls into question the efficacy of performance-based compensation and caused me to leave the post). Yet this lack of awareness of pay also seems to reflect the way that we have come to view money as something others need to think about and perhaps as taking away from the purpose-driven mission that pulls many into this and other service professions.

But when we understand how money works, we are able to make reasonable requests of it. When we fail to understand money, or when we write it off as a "necessary evil," we lose the ability to ask the good questions, much less get the kinds of answers that can help build and strengthen our communities. Money is the developmental talk we need to have with ourselves first, because it frames our choices and values and our views of interdependence. When we understand how finances flow, we truly get how connected we are. We can appreciate our interdependence because we can see it. Leaning into this is a place of dissonance where we can stretch and grow.

The United States as a developmental adolescent has been decidedly uninterested in talking about money in up-close and personal ways. We talk about it in aggregate concepts: loans, minimum wage, national debt. But finding someone who can describe America's money situation with accuracy is as rare as encountering a nonpartisan dialogue today. Isn't that interesting? It's not that money is a boring subject. (In fact, we're scintillated by few things more than by money—what that celebrity makes, how much the neighbor's new car must have cost.) It's that developmentally, we've not been ready to absorb the stories and the perspectives necessary to dwell in those often-fraught spaces of money.

Anytime we encounter something our brain is not ready for, we shut it out. Ignore it. Whole words, people, and systems can be made invisible because we've got no room in the brain's hotel for them. My friend Andrea Burckhard works with life insurance and struggles with this phenomenon. Most people have no spot in their brain for insurance details, so they just shut them out. She produces countless illustrations to help educate customers, but she has found that in the end, it is the fact that they trust her as a person that prompts customer investments rather than an understanding rooted in the products themselves. If her customers could make space for those understandings, they'd likely be thrilled with her choices and amazed at what she is offering. But most just adopt a "she's taking care of me" approach. Our minds shut out what we don't feel ready to absorb. It's not so different from watching a baby sleep through a ton of noise when tired. Our systems are programmed not to overload. (That's an illustration of human development in action.) We see and understand what we are ready to see and comprehend, and those awareness capabilities are built precept on precept. Like learning to crawl before walking, important things happen at each stage of development. They're all good stages, and there's always more to be achieved.

This is part of how we miss so much of what's going on in the world. We literally cannot comprehend it; it requires functions that our brains are not ready to do. A good teacher recognizes when the content has no place to land for students. If a child misses some key lessons on math, that child cannot move on until those precepts are understood. If a teen has no mental scaffold for understanding language, Shakespeare is inaccessible.

Money is a good way to stretch ourselves developmentally. Intuitively, we know this. It's why some kids are given allowances or lawns to mow. We want to teach them to understand the world by teaching them a little about money (and we know those lessons couldn't come from the Tooth Fairy). How things are funded, from whence that funding comes, and how it shapes life in our nation is essential for any citizen to understand. Every endeavor requires resources, and resources always, in some way, involve money. Even the most altruistic, socially progressive endeavor will require money at some stage. But at this moment in time, serious understanding of how money functions remains invisible in most quarters of our adolescent nation.

But there is hope—an emergent awareness on the horizon. The growth of crowdfunding campaigns like those on the GoFundMe platform have been helping us connect the dots. *Money goes here; it's used for that. Without money, we cannot do this.* I give to the bookstore-funding campaign, and the bookstore owner buys shelves for the books. The American millwork company makes the shelves and pays the living wages for thirty-five families, influencing a small community. The bookstore opens and funds ten employee families, along with the people who own the building. I shop at that bookstore and get new books that lead me to do better things. Value on value on value. In these contexts, we no longer see money as evil or magically produced. It is an expression of value (what you offered, made, or contributed) used to create a different value (what you want to do, have, or experience).

Perhaps we can start to learn about money by thinking of it like blood flow in the human body. Like blood flow, money needs to circulate constantly to be really working. And as with blood, if you run out, it is an emergency, requiring a loan from somewhere else. You're hoping that there's a bank with your name on it somewhere close by. You don't want money to pool anywhere in the body (that is what we call inventory—bunches of money sitting around dangerously). Blood pools create problems (strokes, paralysis, and death), and so do money pools when you've got money that stops flowing in your organization for any reason. And if there's a problem where you are losing money, it's like losing blood. It's an emergency, because neither your body nor your business can function long when losing it.

In *The United States of Europe*, reporter and longtime *Washington Post* correspondent T. R. Reid[36] beautifully illustrates the disconnect between money and our adolescent nation. In the opening paragraphs of the book, Reid describes a couple who go on a trip from their home in Buffalo, New York. She works for the local hospital, he for the electric company. They get in their Dodge car, fill up on Amoco gas, add some Quaker oil, and head out to Chicago. In Chicago, they find out what's going on by looking at the *Chicago Sun-Times* and stay at the Holiday Inn, where they enjoy a Mott's apple pie before heading to a Cubs game. With a Verizon phone, they text the kids back home a picture of Dad in his new Brooks Brothers jacket before heading back to Buffalo. Every single thing mentioned in that story—from the gas to the oil, the apple pie to the Cubs ticket—is owned by a European country. That means that the profits from the sales of those things go back to a European nation. Even the power company and hospital at which the husband and wife work, the phone and car they use, and the paper they read are all owned by European companies.

In order to understand our current interdependence—and to frame a declaration of such for ourselves—we must understand how money works.

News Was Never Just News

If government was the proverbial parent in our nation's adolescence, then the newsmakers were our revered/odd/interesting aunts and uncles. Once, we held the news media in childlike awe, believing wholeheartedly in the ideals of unbiased journalism and other noble pursuits. Those who entered the journalistic profession seemingly did so out of a desire to be a part of a public service, part of shaping and offering the truth. The. Truth. As though there is just one version of that.

The bigger problem is that news never actually funded itself in this country. It was always an advertising business that depended heavily on elections to make ends meet. Most small-town newspapers across the country drew as much as 85% of their annual budgets from election spending and the other 15% from other commercial advertising.[37] Subscriptions paid for the distribution but never the work itself. Never.

And then came the internet, where advertisers could see exactly what they were paying for. And in the blink of an internet refresh, all those journalism rules flew out the window in favor of the most sensational ad lines ever written. "You Won't Believe What the Mayor Did Next" or "Smith Family Devastated by Crazed Teacher" or "Should Our Beaches Be Allowed to Show This?"

Media Talk in Maturing America

Understanding the media is deeply connected to understanding how money works. One of the ways we are starting to think about our adulting as a nation is that we are becoming aware that the voices from the air (news, entertainment, edutainment) come from real people. But perhaps more important than understanding that there is a person writing or creating any piece of news or communication we receive is understanding that there is money involved.

Journalism—the craft of unbiased reporting that we expect to give us the facts—is driven by revenue from advertisements. You might even go so far as to say that there is no such thing as a journalism business in this country—that is, no news outlet that is funded 100% by people paying for its journalism. Substack and similar platforms are now providing ways for independent journalists to find their audiences and be paid directly for their writing, but that is still a monetization strategy. Even NPR is funded by a mix of donations, foundations, sponsorships, and government funding. That doesn't mean that the people doing the writing are false or ill-intended. But we all have biases and filters.

We may like to avoid the ads, programming our Tivos to fast-forward through the commercials, but we seem oblivious to the fact that all of our media—by necessity—is monetized by advertisers promoting their products and services. Those products and services, even the political ones we sometimes turn our noses up at, go on to fund jobs we rely on…so that we can buy more products and services. That is how America's world goes 'round!

Between 2005 and 2010, I owned a local online news source with a daily viewership of 10,000 or so people. It was a small operation, but it facilitated an interesting experience. During that time, I spent a lot of my time trying to sell advertising. Interestingly, I had a hard time finding advertisers in our community who could imagine people getting their news online. When I suggested that our advertisers make coupons that folks could use on their phones, the notion was met with a shrug and a dismissal: "That will never happen." Though our news site got twice as many hits per day as the local print newspaper with its 8,000 subscribers, the newspaper got all of the advertising. Our little online news source made 2% of what the newspaper made. I was about three years ahead of schedule and out of sync with the ways the news and advertising have now transformed, but the experience informed much of my understanding of news and advertising.

The local hospital, a city-owned entity at the time, was our only major advertiser. The income from their ads enabled me to pay for the platform service that hosted our free online news and copious pictures. There was no other income. I wanted to deliver unbiased content and produce what I viewed as noble journalism. But when the hospital had a positive event, I felt compelled to report that with beautiful pictures. And when the hospital had a negative event, I would report that, too, but in very careful ways (and maybe not on the front page with a big picture).

I wrote copy for this paper every day while funding my life needs with another work endeavor. The paper required thirty or so hours a week. In that thirty hours, I had to gather information on local crime, big school events, city-council meeting reports, county commission happenings, and more. Most days, I had only a few minutes to gather the content I needed for a story, then maybe half an hour to process the information and grab photos, and another half an hour to write the story. Many times, I felt that I knew very little about the subject. When this was the case, I tried to say so, and yet repeatedly, I'd stand in line at the grocery store and hear someone talking about a story (that only I had reported) as though it were a dissertation-worthy investigative report. I knew it was not.

I also knew that many of our readers just read the captions and looked at pictures. So, often, the picture I chose *was* the story. Usually, the particular angle or vantage point I took the picture from was the only angle I could get, and this could have enormous influence on how the story came across. And there were dozens of choices to make for every story. The power of those choices was daunting, and the responsibility struck me deeply. My stories, created with limited content and even more limited time, were carried on virtually every major news outlet at some point. Associated Press carried them, *Rolling Stone*, CNN, NBC... Knowing how those stories were formed made me uncomfortable, as well as a more aware reader of other news.

When it comes to traditional newspapers that involve getting a subscription, often, readers feel like their subscriptions are funding the newspaper and that, therefore, it is being created for them. They are funding this information. While

Try This: A Personal Exercise to Understand Money Flow

First, try shifting your emotional perspective on money. Do you think it an awful thing? A wonderful thing? Something you need, use, desire, dislike? Or do you have another view? Name your current relationship with and emotional view of money first:

Money is _____.

Whatever your current emotion about money, now try a shift:

Money is _____.

(Insert your own word here, but make it a different idea than your usual one—perhaps even the opposite.)

Now, as an exercise, try proving to yourself that money is the second word you chose. Stretch your own awareness by finding examples in your life and community of money working in a different way or being this different word.

Example:
1. Old idea: "Money is greedy and empty."
2. New idea: "Money is needed and useful."
3. Examples of money being needed and useful: "I have power, I'm warm, etc."

subscriptions certainly help with printing and distribution, the annual budget for the news has always come from advertising, often political advertising. Let's take my local newspaper as an example: 50% of revenues come from political ads, 45% from other advertisements, and 5% from subscriptions. Without political advertising, the *Herald-Citizen* would have folded (pardon the pun) long ago. The rest of the operational funding comes from local and national advertisers. The subscriptions literally fund the circulation effort, but none of the resources, machinery, or reporters required to create the daily paper.

While subscriptions and newspapers remained our main source of news, we could continue to believe in this never-quite-true notion of unbiased journalism (even though the journalists tried). But when the news moved online, the whole dynamic shifted instantly. Suddenly, the advertisers understood the money flow much more clearly than before. They also understood that they could flow instantly from one news source to another with ease. It changed everything about what we called news. Headlines began breaking all journalistic rules in a race for that click. "You Won't Believe What the Mayor Did Last Night" would certainly get more clicks than "Mayor Leads Council Appeal for Parks." Machinery and resources were no longer barriers to entry, and people crowded the field like at a home-game win.

And now we're all reporters, full of bias, in a world where the most obscure writer with the most heavily biased perspective can be easily searched alongside the best-funded, most highly researched piece. If the biased and obscure writer has a better photo, that's the news we use. And then we rail that it is fake and intended to influence for an agenda. Yes, of course it is. It always has been. It's just an exponentially more pronounced dynamic today.

In order to mature as individuals and as a collective, we must first start understanding what our metaphorical allowances mean—how our lives are funded and how the money flows in our worlds. We are not victims of fake news, nor are we living in an incomprehensible money bubble. We can understand these things and, in that understanding, shape how they reflect our values.

Chapter 6

Staying Uncomfortable: Talking Spirituality

CONTINUING ON THE theme of "It's time to talk about these things," let's move to the spirituality talk.

Spirituality—whether it's in the form of organized religion or a more private experience—is something that emerges to the forefront as we mature from adolescence into young adulthood as individuals. Spirituality manifests in many of the same ways on a national level, as well. Look around our adolescent nation and you will find that we are consumed by conversations about purpose, passion, and living our best lives. Indeed, topics like meditation, spirituality, and prayer have moved from niche side chats into mainstream media conversations. While

we may be pressed to put a collective name to our national spirituality, America is definitely "living in the questions."

When I was eighteen years old, it dawned on me that I had only one view of faith: the one in which I had been raised. It seemed to me limiting to accept at face value that I'd been handed the perfect belief system at birth, and so I started exploring. I have a habit of getting into a little too much, and perhaps an illustration of this is in the ways I began exploring faith. A piano and organ player, I played for four services in four different faith structures every Sunday morning from the ages seventeen to twenty-one. I also sang in a band that had a whopping five different belief systems represented within its membership. After that, I lived in a group home in Washington, DC, working for the National 4-H Council, where I had the opportunity to engage in a deep dialogue with a dozen others raised in different belief systems and traditions. The more I explored, the more clearly I could see my beliefs of origin, and the more I came to appreciate how much was still left to understand and know. Those years began a journey that I continue to this day.

For those in ministry and faith-based organizations, this a ripe moment to have deep and genuine conversations that go beyond passing the baton of doctrine. We are a nation of individuals looking for meaning, acceptance, and the kind of faith that can move mountains and build bridges.

In Amish communities, you may have seen the tricked-out buggies blasting all manner of music that are part of the Rumspringa tradition, where young men explore, sow wild oats, and then choose their faith. It's a growing-up thing, this notion of embracing our spirituality and faith. And now we, as a nation heading into a new young-adulthood, are finding faith to be the foundation of all else. If understanding money helps us see the landscape in which we are operating, it is spirituality and faith that give us our reasons for the journey.

We talk much today about being purposeful and passionate. This is the stuff of faith in action. Spirituality takes many forms, and many different types of language are used about it. But at its core, spirituality gets at the essence of identity: "Who am I, why am I, and what am I to be?" We humans around the globe share a yearning for answers to these questions, for a spiritual foundation. It's perhaps easy to understand why so many of us maintain the spiritual tradition we were handed by our immediate family and culture without questioning. These questions are so big that we get fearful and subsequently angry when someone questions what we've chosen to believe.

Today, we are getting at those spiritual conversations through political wars, where some of us feel like we are deep in the trenches of a battle, others of us feel frightened to speak our thoughts, and still others of us find relative shelter in political homelessness. The polarization and fear factors aren't helping us move forward in shaping our spiritual understandings.

We're back to that anger, aren't we? People sitting together in pews every Sunday have started to feel like strangers, loved ones at the dinner table like enemies. Toxic political dialogue, hate-filled rants on social media, and agenda-driven news stories have become the new norm.

But books and podcasts like Sarah Stewart Holland and Beth Silvers's *I Think You're Wrong (But I'm Listening): A Guide to Grace-Filled Political Conversations*[38] are helping us move toward the dialogues that we need in order to sort ourselves out and get serious about shaping our beliefs. Sarah and Beth are two working moms from opposite ends of the political spectrum who contend that there is a better way. They believe that we can choose to respect the dignity of every person, choose to recognize that issues are nuanced and can't be reduced to political talking points, choose to listen in order to understand, and choose gentleness and patience. In their podcast *Pantsuit Politics*, they illustrate that people from opposing perspectives can have calm, grace-filled conversations by putting relationships and understanding before argument. Emily Freeman, *The Wall Street Journal* writer and author of *The Next Right Thing,* describes the project like this: "Sarah from the left and Beth from the right serve as our guides through conflict and complexity, delivering us into connection. I wish every person living in the United States would read this compelling book, from the youngest voter to those holding the highest office."

Following the norm of late adolescence, we are a nation trying to articulate our beliefs and find our spiritual path forward so that we may choose all the rest. For those in ministry and faith-based organizations, this is a ripe moment to have deep and genuine conversations that go beyond passing the baton of doctrine. We are a nation of individuals looking for meaning, acceptance, and the kind of faith that can move mountains and build bridges. We need conversations, information, historical perspective, rich experiences, and a good dose of the real. We need genuine relationships and faith that moves beyond where we sit on a Sunday and into how we live on a Tuesday afternoon.

Doing that work is hard and requires that we move out of the cliquish comforts of our teenage crew. As we talk about creating safe spaces to decide what we believe, spirituality must be at the center of the conversation.

We will do this one of two ways. In maturational terms, we'll choose a faith system, because that's what happens at this age. Intentional or accidental, we will nationally adopt some form of revised belief system that represents this country.

But if you cast your mind back to earlier in the book, where we talked about hierarchical development, you'll recall that our development doesn't have to be automatic and passive. We can make deliberate, growth-oriented decisions.

There are choices within choices here—not only what we believe, but why we believe that and what we want to do with that belief system. As we head into a new young-adulthood, it is time for us to choose our faith. Like Ben Franklin's chosen virtues, our own Declarations of Interdependence will reflect our faith and value choices.

American theologian James Fowler describes faith as making meaning.[39] Fowler, who was known for his theory of the stages of faith development, argues that humans try to order our lives by answering the big questions about meaning and purpose. He also suggests that faith is different than religion. We may develop our faith within a religious affiliation, but they are not one and the same. Everyone has a faith—some kind of belief system— in order to function. More than a cognitive element, our use of the word *faith* in this context is analogous to our use of the word *heart* or *soul*. It describes the indescribable and intangible, but very real, essence of ourselves.

Faith Development Stages	
Experienced	Stage 0—Undifferentiated Faith
	Stage 1—Intuitive-Projective Faith
	Stage 2—Mythic-Literal Faith
Socialized	Stage 3—Synthetic-Conventional Faith
Searching	Stage 4—Individuative-Reflective Faith
Integrative	Stage 5—Conjunctive Faith
	Stage 6—Universalizing Faith

In Fowler's studies, faith development is seen as age-related but not age-guaranteed or age-specific in individuals. His stages are therefore not things that come with age (maturational development) but the kind of growth that comes with spiritual intention (hierarchical development). Fowler's research found that most people do advance through initial faith stages over about eighteen years, but many never move from that spot. There's a wall in spiritual development that is rarely breached. The question for us, then, is how we will breach this wall.

The inspirational M. Scott Peck[40]— author of the classic *The Road Less Traveled*—simplified Fowler's six-stage model into four stages of faith.

The first, the chaotic-antisocial level, is where beliefs are undifferentiated and unorganized into any sort of coherent system for the individual. This is followed in Peck's model by the more formalized institutional faith, where an established belief system (i.e.,

a doctrinal statement) makes up the basis of one's personal statement of faith. In stage three, institutional views are upended and questioned, and the individual seeks a personally crafted statement of belief and faith for themself based on their studies and experiences. Finally, the individual moves to the fourth stage, where the previous-stage learnings are integrated and people accept questions of faith, mysteries, or paradox without fear. This stage emphasizes community as well as individual concerns.

I invite you to ask yourself the question, "Where am I as an individual?" Don't get too caught up in definitions of faith; instead, think about your faith as you define it, and as you do, try to suspend the urge to judge yourself, giving yourself a quick thumbs up or thumbs down.

It may be easier to think about our collective faith stage. Which stage are we in as a country? Are we in a space of undifferentiated disorganization, like in the first stage? Or have we reached the level of institutional faith represented by the second stage, or even the questioning of the third? Or is there a chance we've arrived at the fourth stage—the stage of integration and fearlessness? (I have an opinion, but the act of inviting you to think about it is more valuable than my offer of opinion.)

The act of asking and answering this question—"Where is my faith now?"—is likely to be rife with dissonance as well as discovery. Faith, like money, is an uncomfortable topic. Intuitively, we feel much is at stake.

In our fear of getting it wrong, we often wrap up our faith like a box and put a bow on it. *There. Done.* It is ever so much more peaceful that way. Or so it seems. (I'm reminded of the joke where a wife comments to her husband that he hasn't said he loves her in years. The husband responds that he told her already. Once. If anything changes, he'll let her know.)

Our faith is a relationship, and like any relationship, it requires that we get it out of that neat box and let it grow. There seems to be such fear of doing so. I find myself hesitant even to bring it up. But fear is the underbelly of anger and defense. It is not conducive to our growth. When it comes to our faith, some of us have learned just enough to be frightened, which makes us rather scary, because fear often makes us defensive, aggressive, or destructive toward ourselves or others.

When growing our own spirituality, perhaps the metaphor of a tree is better: something that is rooted and fixed, but growing ever deeper and taller, branching, bearing fruit, and becoming shade for others. Fowler's and Peck's depictions of faith represent a journey of growth. Every stage has beauty and value, and reaching higher and deeper is a rich quest.

These two subjects—spirituality and money—may be sufficient dissonant fodder for your individual or group deliberation. But should you be ready for other subjects, there are a host of practical and existential topics to explore as a maturing person interested in a maturing nation. Relationships and sexuality, identity and roles, health and environment, community and the well-being of all, learning, career, and family, purpose and contribution: these are among the many topics and interests that a young person has to sort out, and our country is right on the edge of all of them.

The truth is that our finest moments are most likely to occur when we are feeling deeply uncomfortable, unhappy, or unfulfilled. For it is only in such moments, propelled by our discomfort, that we are likely to step out of our ruts and start searching for different ways or truer answers.
—M. Scott Peck

Chapter 7

Development with Intention: How Shared Crisis Can Help Us Build

IF YOU'VE READ this far, then by now, you understand that maturational development follows a predictable path. Now that we've arrived at that "young adult" stop, we are making decisions that will likely frame the kind of young adult nation we'll be for the next 240 years or so.

It may sound strange to say, but as I write this (at the end of 2020), I have never been more excited about living in this country. This moment is ripe. It is juicy with opportunity and edgy with desire. The COVID-19 virus was met with choruses of "We're in this together" and people stumbling over themselves to be thoughtful, careful, and kind as businesses and individuals. The tragedies leading to the Black Lives Matter protests[41] were met with people flooding the bookstores and libraries (as well as the streets) in search of information, historical perspective, and a how-to manual for their next steps. We are in the midst of a shared crisis, which means, should we choose it, we are also in the midst of a great opportunity for growth.

Before we dive into the dissonance of these crises in more depth, let's take a moment to frame where we are.

A Graduation Speech for America

If we are America's graduating class of seniors ("we" meaning all of us, at every age), then our commencement speech might sound something like this:

Dear America, Class of the 2020s,

In these moments of upheaval and shared concern, you've got a lot going for you. You have assets.

You believe in yourselves. You are confident. You cannot fail because you believe you cannot fail.

You are spiritual. You are interested in purpose and in being a generation that matters not just for this moment, but for the next few hundred years. You see the wrongs, and you want to find ways to make them right. There may be many things you do not understand fully yet: faith, family, finances, media, or manners. But you know you are missing at least a few of those, and you're after learning. You're all about learning. You have the confidence to learn and grow.

And right now, that confidence—that boldness of youth—is exactly what you need to face these obstacles.

Be patient with yourselves. Try to be kind to each other and to the planet. Take manners seriously. As Lady Mary Montagu[42] put it, "Civility costs nothing and buys everything." Say please and thank you. Be that change that you want to see. Give that person across from you a reason to smile. If you have a reason to smile, you're better poised to reason together.

Be intentional, because right now, a little intention has the capacity to create a tsunami of success. We will together imagine a country that we want to live in twenty-five years from now, a hundred years from now. And, acting together, we will create that country.

Here's the thing: You will grow up, America. It's unavoidable. Literally and figuratively (thanks to the hormones in our foods[43]), the Civil War uniform of our childhood no longer fits. The choice before us is one of determining the level to which we will engage in growth with intention. Do we become better through growing together? Or declare that this bird cannot change?

Though the years will force physiological changes for ourselves and for our society, the kind of people and society we become is largely determined by the ways we choose to grow.

Growth sounds easy. But not everyone who changes grows. Because growth is also really hard. It's hard as an individual. And it's equally hard as a country.

The quest for learning and growth poses the very real danger that everything will change. When we develop, our thinking, emotional capacities, and worldviews will change. Different things will be funny to us. Different things will seem interesting. We'll have different views and different ways of knowing than we possessed when we began. Those differences will matter not only to us, but to every relationship in our lives.

Choosing development—or any significant learning endeavor—means making shifts that will alter our ways of knowing. It will change our relationships, whether or not we want it to. It will change our views, our faith, our politics, and our ways of living and working and contributing together. It will change everything.

You aren't ready for that. No one is. But it's in you. In the deepest ways that you know anything at all, you know that you need to keep learning. You know that you were designed for this quest.

You know that we'll be better if we take the pottery wheel and shape the cup from which we want to drink for this nation's next 240 years.

Let's explore what it means to grow with intentionality. Let's identify our teachers, our guardians, and our facilitators in this national journey. Let's embark on a path that helps us transition into the exciting realm of young adulthood with a sense of promise and prosperity.

This is our time to choose our career paths, to consider the nature of our communities and neighborhoods, to dream and become. This is a time to shine, and that is possible with a bit of awareness and focus as a country.

You are surrounded by teachers that are centuries old. They have left you insights and treasures in their books. This is part of your inheritance. Receive it. Pursue those treasures. A good read leads to reflection, perspective shifts, development, and ultimately, a richer sense of self. After you read, talk about those insights together. Don't miss that part—we need each other to frame our explorations and actions. Understand our interdependence and the ways that our friends, our communities, and even those writers weave a fabric that is our flag and promise today. That is my hope for you, individually, and for us—teenage America moving into adulthood and our next 240 years.

Chapter 8

The Nature of Intentional Growth

MAYBE YOU'VE NOTICED: people get older, but they don't necessarily grow wiser. Some folks leave this plane of existence having met the maturational development milestones but otherwise pretty much as they were at eleven or twelve, in terms of their thinking or emotional capabilities.

Have you wondered why, given similar circumstances and resources and even personalities, some people seem to possess intellectual, emotional, and spiritual capacities that others lack?

Identical twins raised in the same home and circumstances, offered the same resources and seemingly similar life experiences, and with similar IQs and mental capacities can be worlds apart in their thinking, feeling, and spiritual expression.

Our years don't tell the whole story, do they?

A seventy-eight-year-old woman who has lived in poverty her whole life can be a wise woman or one that behaves like a child. A sixty-five-year-old man can be pretty much the same selfish teen he was decades ago or a great coach and mentor. A fifty-year-old can be a productive and influential part of society or as attention-seeking as the neediest nine-year-old. A person can celebrate their thirty-fifth birthday in full awareness of broad questions of personal responsibility or in egocentric awareness only of himself.

One adult person can face a life-ending diagnosis, financial impoverishment, public embarrassment, familial discord, and the stress of a thousand arrows with equanimity and philosophical calm. Their response to all of that stress and misfortune: some productive endeavor, such as growing companies or trees or relationships.

Another adult can simply imagine the possibility of one of their healthy children becoming infected by a virus amid familial, financial, and physical stability and lose their ability to function at all.

What creates these kinds of differences in response? Psychologists have been asking that question for a long time. And understanding the answer is one key to understanding how to move ourselves, and our communities and country, forward in positive ways.

When we show someone suffering in some capacity, we think that most people will be able to empathize with their perspective. But our understanding of psychology suggests otherwise. While some people can identify a relatable personal perspective—something similar that they have experienced—the majority of us cannot imagine a situation that we have not directly lived. In my early studies with developmentalist Dr. Roger Aubrey[45] at Peabody College, this point was made repeatedly: research shows that an estimated 75% of the population of the United States functions in Piaget's concrete operations at an egocentric level. That means that most of us can only understand a thing

Jean Piaget in Ann Arbor

Developmental theorists have long noted that our development is a thing differentiated from other aspects of personality, like intelligence and strengths.

Jean Piaget is one of the most famous of these theorists and is referenced heavily here for his differentiation of what he called concrete and formal operations—literality and abstraction, among other variables.

He noted that these developmental shifts were age-related but not age-specific or age-guaranteed.[44]

as we understand our own feelings and thoughts. Most of us can see only our own feelings and thoughts. "I lost a parent, too" or "I felt so scared when I went to court" or "I was devastated when I heard about the cancer."

When we speak of distances created because of dramatically different life

Try This: Hierarchical Development and How to Think More Abstractly

The kind of development that is chosen is called *hierarchical development*, and it doesn't come automatically as we age. The term refers to the idea that there is a hierarchy—think of it like a set of stairs—in expanding our ability to think, feel, and consider differences.

Very few people are total concrete thinkers. Even those who have mental impairments will have some abstract thinking. It's a spectrum. The average person could learn how to think abstractly even more. One way to do so is to talk to more people. Learn their perspectives and try to empathize with them. As the cliché goes, you walk a mile in their shoes.

Think of this as a mental muscle. Here are some exercises.

Alone: Read about people who are different than you, people with wildly different experiences and worldviews. Watch movies and shows about people who are different than you and listen to understand them, not to agree or disagree with them.

With others: State your intention in exercising this muscle. As others speak, resist the urge to tell your own related story, exploring more of theirs instead. Restate, ask, and listen deeply. Adopt this as a discipline and enjoy all you learn!

experiences and the chasm of misunderstanding that lies between us, we are speaking of the need for perspective-taking and the frustration that some are able to do that while others cannot.

If you can step inside another's thoughts or feelings, then realize that you are in the minority, the 25% of our US population that has moved into Piaget's formal operations with the ability to perspective-take, use metaphor, and experience real empathy. To recall our exploration of maturational development, the first part of getting stronger as a country is an awareness of "We are here."

Some of our separations and natural divides come from our need for more Americans to move from concrete into formal operations (to choose development) and embrace our maturity beyond the egocentric state (everything is about me and my experience). The fact that this book is of interest to you is evidence that you have done or are doing both of those and can support others in the same kind of growth.

Let's move on and explore this idea of formal operations in a little more depth. (We'll call it perspective-taking to make communication a little clearer.)

Perspective-Taking and Hierarchical Development

Instinctively, most of us actually try to promote and learn abstraction and perspective-taking whether we realize it or not. When raising children who misbehave, parents can often be heard saying things like: "How do you think Sarah felt when you destroyed her art?" or "How do you think Joe feels when you make all of the decisions in the game?" These questions promote abstract thinking and perspective-taking. Cultivating the ability to perspective-take is one step of hierarchical development. Like all hierarchical development, it's not automatic—like maturational

Try This: Perspective-Taking Exercise

Essential to our interdependence and intentional growth is really understanding the perspective of another without projecting our own experience onto them. That's tough. Here's an exercise to try to stretch and strengthen that capability.

Expanding on the previous exercise, with a friend or partner, try having a conversation in which you only ask questions for fifteen minutes. Once you have that down, try moving toward thirty minutes. Only questions. No statements. "How did that make you feel? What happened next? What did they say? What do you plan to do? What are you thinking? What kind of support did you get?"

It may feel odd to you, but my experience is that (if I can manage the self-discipline) my friend doesn't even notice. And I learn a lot. About *them*. And it feels good to both of us.

development—or age-specific. A child of seven can easily be in a higher developmental stage of thinking than an adult of fifty-seven, regardless of IQ.

Consider this as it relates to big, thorny issues like race, equity, abuse, or neglect. We have a profound developmental disconnect. What makes certain actions obvious to a minority of the population may remain quite invisible to the majority. This is not something that can be legislated, mandated, or easily taught.

If we aspire to be more as a country, I believe we have to do more than develop well on the maturational scale; we need to tackle hierarchical development, of which the ability to perspective-take is just one example.

Perspective-taking is necessary in order to grasp the concept of interdependence. Independence is easy—we all have that one. But interdependence is a much taller order in developmental terms. And we have a long way to go.

Not too long ago, I happened onto the posting of an old friend from childhood on Facebook. She had written what she called a "rant" about her rights as a white, southern, Gen-X woman who refused "to be shamed and apologize for the way God created me." As I read her angry-sounding words, I was filled with incredulity and frustration. *This is not about you*, I thought. I wondered what had prompted her message to the masses. It seemed highly unlikely that she'd been accosted or hassled by anyone in our small town about her whiteness, southern-ness, or Gen-X age. So where was this heat coming from?

In the way of social media, a little curious clicking led me to her daughter's page. Then I read her daughter's long post from a couple of years ago, in which the daughter recounted her experience in Boston working in a downtown community-development project. She was riding in a car with three friends, Black men from her gym, who were headed to a celebration where their months of hard work would be recognized with a certification. On their way, the daughter was pulled over by police. No reason was given for the stop. She was not asked to produce her license or registration. And while she was never asked to leave the car or given an explanation for the stop, the men were removed, questioned for a long time, thoroughly searched, and humiliated. The police asked her repeatedly if she was okay and if she was driving with these men by choice. When the friends were returned to the car (without charges), they completed their drive in devastated silence. The daughter's head was spinning as she tried to make sense of what had just happened. And they had been delayed so much that they missed the testing and certification opportunity for which they'd worked so hard. The daughter felt their situation deeply and wanted to do something about it. So she wrote a post on Facebook to document the experience for others to see. A credible witness to her friends and family, she felt her message could be heard and perhaps help reshape a society where this type of thing can happen, does happen, and did happen in her world.

Hundreds of miles away, the mother in this situation is an intelligent, articulate, passionate, well-read woman who has raised a daughter capable of perhaps more developmental perspective than she—capable of abstraction and perspective-taking. Mother cannot imagine daughter's perspective (let alone the perspective of the three Black men in the story). She just can't get her head around it. Instead, in the mother's Facebook post, we witness her return to her own experience, seemingly removed from her daughter's reality, where perhaps she reached the conclusion that her only way to participate with the post was to see herself as being shamed for being white, Gen-X, and southern. Is that where the heat for her "rant" was sparked? Had it been smoldering for a couple of years?

We are a teenage nation, and most of us are inexorably tethered to our own perspectives. It's hard for us to respond to any crisis or concern held by someone else without putting them in our shoes. What an opportunity stories like this represent! I imagine a lot of love and respect between these two women, and I imagine an ability to navigate, with focus, the idea that understanding the perspectives of three Black men in Boston is truly about the men in Boston. And while even our best urge is to move in and say, "What can I do to help?" let's not rush that process. We'll quickly revert to our own perspectives and life experiences and risk dismissing theirs in the process.

Since the mother is articulate and intelligent, with her intention and willingness, there is a high possibility of success if she works to understand her daughter's perspective. Fundamentally, she loves her daughter and respects her. The mother has taught the daughter to value intentional growth, and the daughter has learned those lessons well. This upcoming generation that we've fed and taught about perspectives may in turn have ways of stretching their parents' thinking for the good of us all.

As we develop with intention, we're trying to build a shared awareness of where we are and how we are alike and different so that we can piggyback on one another's strengths. There is a beautiful model called the Clifton Strengths that captures individuals' natural talents and inherent strengths outside of developmental functioning. I've found this a good and powerful way to move toward developmental shifts: focusing on feeding the strengths. As we think about getting into perspective-taking, this model seems an encouraging place to start.

The Clifton Strengths Model

The global strengths-based psychology movement (a forerunner to the positive psychology movement) started six decades ago when psychologist and educator Donald O. Clifton posed a simple question: "What would happen if we studied what was right with people versus what's wrong with people?"

When Clifton, who served in the US Air Force, returned from World War II, he felt that he had seen enough of war and wanted to spend the rest of his life doing good for humankind. This desire fed an intense interest in studying human development. Clifton began his research at the University of Nebraska-Lincoln library, where he was struck that all of the psychology books he could find were about what was wrong with people. He couldn't find a single one about what might be right with people. The rest is history.[46]

Through his research, Clifton distilled thirty-four strengths along with a formula that captures this profound concept in a simple fashion: Talent x Investment = Strength.

Talents, Clifton wrote, are your "naturally recurring patterns of thought, feeling, or behavior." They're the innate, natural abilities you can productively apply. "To turn those talents into strengths, you must *invest* in them—practice using them and add *knowledge* and *skills* to them." Using 177 questions, the Clifton Strengths test is designed to unlock the true you, challenging you to become the best you.

Seeing a top-five list of strengths was an empowering experience for me—not just because of what they were, but also because it gave me permission to let go of being great at all thirty-four things. It prompted me to let go of managing the sales team because I am not as good at managing and arranging as Dave. And with his support, it gave me the opportunity to live more in the world of strategy, thinking longer-term about our business. If I focus on cultivating my top five, it feels good—easy, even.

Your strengths are one in 33 million.

One in 33 million: those are the rough odds that someone shares the exact same themes or "Top 5 Strengths" as you or me, so this test offers a relatively unique profile.

We are probably not going to be immediately successful in getting out of our own way in perspective-taking and growth.

The quest is like trying to use the less dominant hand to write. But if we start our path of intentional growth from a position of investing in our talents, we are starting from a position of strength.

According to Clifton, people grow more and faster by developing their strengths than by trying to mitigate their weaknesses.

Dave and I have taken this to heart and restructured our work together based on the results of our strength profiles. The result has been profound and immediate. I feel free, and he feels respected and valued for the things he brings. And the business results have exponentially facilitated both success and growth. We've given the strengths test to our colleagues, friends, and family, and we find immediate traction and consistent references with little debriefing or discussion about the results.

The Clifton research[47]—now decades strong—indicates that your greatest room for overall personal improvement isn't where you're weakest, but rather where you're strongest. As we look to grow with intention, this seems a powerful and productive place to start.

America and Literacy

If you were to ask most Americans on the street today whether literacy remains a big issue in the United States, you'd be met with mostly nos. It seems like a problem of the past or that one that exists "out there."

If you had polled me several years ago, I would have been one of those nos. Now, I would tell you something different.

When I was hiring a large number of people for a manufacturing work expansion for my and Dave's company, I worked with the state to help find candidates using a process called the Career Readiness Certification (CRC). The CRC measures reading (at about a second-grade level), math, and the ability to follow instructions and problem-solve, particularly for maker jobs in manufacturing.[48]

To get a benchmark, I tested fifteen solid employees—not the strongest, but fully able to achieve objectives—to see their level of achievement on the instrument. The CRC certifies at Bronze, Silver, and Gold levels. The associates I tested demonstrated a Silver or Gold level of achievement, which means satisfactory in at least two of the three areas scored. This is not a GED-level (high-school-equivalency-level) test. This test requires far less than that.

We tested almost 1,200 persons that year for the openings and found only 412 who could pass the CRC at a Gold or Silver level. Those results—that just 30% of our candidates were capable of reading at a second-grade level—so astounded us that we tested our entire workforce of 300-plus persons to see where the reading level was. We found that, within the existing workforce, some 35% were reading below a second-grade level and about 12% could not read at all. With few exceptions, all these employees had a high school diploma or equivalent. They had family, community, and work roles that they filled responsibly. But they were not literate. We immediately started working with the state to bring in reading and math workshops as

Try This:
Discuss These Stats on Literacy

Literacy is not just the literal ability to read. It also includes the ability to perform the activities of daily living, from getting gas with a credit card to filling out an application online. The article "Illiteracy in America" by Rebecca Lake[49] consolidates a number of sources and compiles a list of twenty-three surprising statistics, which include:

32 million adults in America are considered to be illiterate; about 14% of the entire adult population cannot read. Among developed nations, the United States ranks 16th for adult reading.

Between 40 and 44 million adults (roughly 23% of the US) are limited to reading below basic proficiency levels (below second grade). Some 30 million adults aren't able to comprehend texts written for ten-year-olds. Just 11% of men and 12% of women make the grade as proficient readers.

Literacy is critical to all other forms of knowledge: math, science, problem-solving, farming, and more. And illiteracy is linked to trouble with the law and with poverty: 85% of youths in juvenile court are considered functionally illiterate. As many as 75% of welfare recipients struggle to read the simplest texts. This makes literacy a core quality-of-life and economic concern, and an estimated $225 billion is lost in productivity each year due to literacy needs.

education or navigate medical processes when one can't read and fully absorb all of the information needed. Add to that the fact that so much of our work is increasingly thought work—you can't even apply for unemployment in this country without computer literacy.

Now consider the ramifications of low literacy in combination with the fact that most of our country works in concrete operations, where abstraction is difficult or impossible and perspective-taking and true empathy are highly unlikely. No wonder videos are so popular. No wonder we only read headlines and find the simplest and briefest of tweets to be comprehensible. No wonder folks look for solace in like-talking cliques where they seek feelings of safety and show their fear with the face of hate.

If we're going to move our country in the direction of interdependence—considering the integrated needs of all, moving beyond systemic fear, and shaping policies that incorporate the ways money and people and values work together—we've got to learn to read. Increasing literacy across the country is one of our biggest opportunities today.

we absorbed all of the ramifications of this information. I pondered how frightening it must be to go through life unable to read above a second-grade level. How intimidating to try to guide children through an

Chapter 9

What Development Can Give You

L ET'S DIAL THE conversation back to you. What do you want to improve about your world? What do you want to fix in your relationships and your life? How are your choices working out for you now? How do you feel about money and your management of it, about your understanding of how it flows in your world? How are you feeling about your spiritual development and daily movement? And how do you decide what you think?

We're back to the question that started this book: How do we decide what we think?

So far, we've talked about why that question is on our minds at all: we've got a lot of shared crises to navigate together. We need the space and framework to put our own thoughts in order.

We've also talked about the ways that we can view this current moment as a maturational developmental shift for our country: moving from an America that looks and acts a lot like a teenager to an America that looks and acts like a young adult. We've looked at the evidence linking how we've behaved nationally for the past fifty years with analogous perspectives of an individual teen. We've seen how our entertainment, our musical culture, and our views of money and spirituality have reflected a progression analogous to that of a maturing teenager.

And we've discussed how—bidden or unbidden—we're moving as a country into that space of young adulthood, where questions of career, family, faith, community, money, and spirituality will come together. In young adulthood, the concrete is still wet. We can write anything in it, make it any shape we like.

But in the next few years, our concrete is going to set. Anything we change will be harder and require more deliberate force.

That's what makes this moment in American history so exciting. We are in the wet-concrete stage, shaping our next couple hundred years. How we manage the maturational tasks thrust upon us as we age nationally will determine our levels of satisfaction and happiness as well as success.

But we're not finished simply by managing the things that come inevitably with our years. We must consider hierarchical development, which is not automatic but chosen, which requires effort and true intention but leads to the really sweet stuff.

In the following pages, we'll go deeper into that intentional kind of development and what's necessary to pursue it. We'll talk about the changes we choose and how they lead to both the most difficult and the best experiences. And finally, we'll outline a way to go about this development as an individual, small group, or community.

What development can do for you is help you answer your own questions and move in the ways that matter most to you right now. We are talking about *you* choosing to grow *you*, moving toward what matters to *you*.

We've touched on it briefly, but now we're going to expand on what hierarchical development is.

What Exactly Is Hierarchical Development?

We could get pretty deep into the weeds by going into hierarchical developmental theory. That kind of depth is best left for another book. Instead, I'm going to outline the brass tacks, so that we will be on the same page and speaking the same language going forward.

Here are the main things that you need to know about growing your capacities for emotion, thought, and understanding with intention—all those things that are hallmarks of hierarchical development:

- It is possible for everyone.
- It is different than intelligence.
- It changes the ways we think and learn and know—permanently.
- It is necessary for the development of societies and families, where the ability to understand each other and communicate and build things together is important.

Why should you want to develop with intention? Isn't it good enough to deal with the kind of growth and change that comes with age—both for ourselves and for the country?

I like to think of hierarchical development like climbing a mountain. It takes a lot of intentional effort, but when you reach the top, everything you see—and the way you feel—is totally transformed.

Dave and I live on a small mountain (okay, it's a hill) that I climb often. But even with a lower elevation, the impact is similar: when I look up into the forest's trees, my spirit lifts, and I see and feel things differently. I feel transformed in some way. When we look out at the vista of trees, we are inspired to have bigger thoughts and visions. The world seems smaller and bigger at the same time. We have a relationship with the landscape that makes new things believable and possible. We are filled with gratitude and perspective.

Another apt analogy is having children. I've watched loved ones have children. It doesn't just change some things. For most of them, those who grab the experience with both hands and all of their intention, it changes everything. How they sleep is different; how they think about media, entertainment, food, and their own house is different. And it's not just different for a second or two—it's the kind of change that transforms for life.

And not everyone seeks that, just like not everyone longs to be a mountaineer. But those that do say it is unimaginably rewarding. That, friends, is the stuff of chosen development. It can be as relatively unobtrusive as climbing a mountain or as life-changing as having a child. It is the kind of development that seemingly restructures nearly every neurological pathway.

The point here isn't that we should all go off and have children or climb Mt. Everest. Rather, what I mean to suggest is that life is richer when we reach for things that push us, that require us to rewire and reboot, body and soul. Hierarchical development is like that.

Having a child is a particularly good metaphor, because you can see how that

Differentiating Human Intelligence from Human Development

Developed by Michael Commons and built on by others since the 1980s, the the model of hierarchical complexity, or MHC,[50] differentiates human intelligence from human development.

Intelligence is marked by complex cognitive feats and high levels of motivation and self-awareness.

Intelligence enables humans to remember descriptions of things and use those descriptions in future behaviors. It is a cognitive process. It gives humans the cognitive abilities to learn, form concepts, understand, and reason, including the capacities to recognize patterns, innovate, plan, solve problems, and employ language to communicate.

Intelligence enables humans to experience and think.

Development enables humans to use those experiences and think in a variety of ways. It enables them to see more and more deeply—to discern nuances. Development is marked by the ability to craft a different lens for viewing and thinking, for consideration and decision-making.

Development enables humans to discern and decide and to think differently.

development makes all of your relationships different. Different things are funny; different things are interesting. It may be difficult to relate to those who haven't shared the experience.

This is true for all types of chosen development, which is very much interlinked with the experiences we choose and the ways we embrace our transformation within them.

So, can you achieve this kind of development? Can your loved ones?

Yes, we all can. Everyone can develop, but it requires a lot of effort, and not everyone is willing to expend that. There are also talents and strengths that come into play.

Hierarchical development is different than intelligence. Intelligence describes the ability to process and recall information. Having a lot of intelligence is like having a really fast computer. Hierarchical development, in computer terms, would be analogous to AI—the ability to expand knowledge from one area to anticipate and extrapolate into others.

Start Where You Are

This all might make you wonder, "Where am I right now?" The answer is that it doesn't really matter. You are where you are. The awareness that there are other ways of knowing accessible to you is enough to move you forward and up your own personal mountains. With each step, there will be new vistas and new comprehensions.

When you raise children, no one can tell you how you're going to develop, and you would be hard-pressed to know how to put words to the shifts that occur inside you along the way. What matters to me, even as a developmentalist, is not naming these shifts so much as always pursuing a wider vista and a better view of those with whom I share this planet.

I don't feel prepared in this moment to write a Declaration of Interdependence. I don't feel prepared in this moment to embrace shared crisis to build a better us

or a better US. But I do know that I can develop and that I can learn about these things. I know that my development—and yours—is necessary in order to have a successful society. It's necessary in order to even define what that means.

There are many thinkers concerned about our future from a developmental perspective. I am not the only one to worry that, as we increasingly rely on technology that we cannot see or hold in our hands, the intelligent literal (concrete) thinker could be left behind. Robert Kegan[51] is a developmental psychologist, author, and former professor at Harvard's Graduate School of Education. Along with fellow psychologist Lisa Laskow Lahey, Kegan has written about something he calls the "Immunity Map,"[52] which is a system for measuring the gap between our intentions or goals and our actions, as well as identifying the hidden roadblocks. Kegan and Lahey's work intends to help communities and individuals overcome their immunity to change by identifying behaviors and attitudes that are standing in their way.

We naturally resist change, even when we think we are seeking it. It's not personal; it's biological. Our brains are wired to go down the same neural pathways so that we can navigate life without unwittingly stepping into danger or becoming overwhelmed by endless choices and options.

From birth, we're programed to shut out what we don't need. As infants, we responded to the sound of a mother or other caregiver but learned to sleep through other sounds. At work, we're able to shut out the sounds of others in the office, a conversation down the hall, or cars going by on the street. As we concentrate on a book, the sounds of birds chirping or children playing outside dissolve away.

Hierarchical development—development by choice—involves working hard to defeat the very systems that protect us in order to find a new and improved awareness.

It requires dissonance—that thing that is grating, uncomfortable, or doesn't fit. We don't like dissonance. It makes us edgy and ill at ease. But we need it. Dissonance is the sandpaper that produces a smooth finish. Without dissonance, we would never have learned to walk. At some point, there had to be that thing that we wanted that was out of reach, that object of desire that made us decide to crawl or, later, to pull ourselves up onto a couch.

Have you ever watched a newly born foal stand for the first time? It's a tough sight. The young horse, minutes old, gets those gangly, shaking legs under him and pushes up. It looks pretty dicey, but eventually, it happens. Then he teeters over to the mare, looking for that first drink. She doesn't move over to him. He takes one, then two, then three shaky steps and at last makes it to sustenance! As he reaches for that milk, the mare moves away. Now, that seems cruel to an average bystander. But look more closely, and you'll see that it's a thing of developmental beauty. The new foal takes a few more steps, and Momma may move away again or let him take a few sips. But she keeps him moving to stretch him, because the dissonance of unreachable desire is, from birth, serving to strengthen and feed us.

Dissonance is always involved in development. If we want to grow beyond simple maturational milestones, if we want to excel or think our biggest thoughts or even have a really good way of continually deciding what we know, we have to be okay with dissonance.

We are designed for stability. For ease. We are creatures of habit, from our regular parking space to "our" seat in our house to the particular way we open a bottle. In this way, chosen development at an individual level is counterintuitive. It requires us to push past that voice deep within that says, "Resist crisis, resist change."

But, in fact, crises are not things to lament, but moments of dissonance that we can embrace if we're interested in true growth: change by choice. This is true for private crises—divorce, loss of a job, or major illness—and societal crises—a pandemic, economic depression, or the exposure of police brutality.

We don't actually have to seek out dissonance. It finds us daily. But usually, we ignore it, either by tuning it out or by rejecting it in anger. During the COVID-19 pandemic, many felt overwhelmed by the initial dissonance of the information about the dangers. Quickly, that dissonance became too uncomfortable for many—too many voices, too difficult to know what I think, too much to take in. So, we witnessed many that rejected the idea of COVID-19 entirely and grew frustrated with masked reminders of the dissonance.

Perhaps you've witnessed a child or young person, frustrated by their inability to complete a task or problem, feeling overwhelmed by dissonance and rejecting the whole exercise in anger. When the challenge becomes too hard, we become fearful. We experience a kind of brain pain—a discomfort—that makes us want to shake off the whole frustrating object or topic.

When we express gratitude for everything—every single thing—then we can pull that dissonance in and continue our developmental process. When we acknowledge the things that are causing us fear or pain or the things about which we feel helpless—and do so with gratitude for the growth opportunity it provides us—we settle down. We change the chemistry in our bodies from the loads of fight-or-flight adrenaline and stress-managing cortisol to the helpful hormones.

I can't think of something we call a crisis that isn't considered a really bad thing. When we think "crisis," we think loss, pain, uncertainty, confusion, helplessness, or anger. But the crisis that lands in our inbox or on our doorstep, that takes the life of a loved one or that destroys our home or business—that crisis has real transformative power within us.

In her book *The Hate U Give*, author Angie Thomas[53] creates Starr, a teenage girl who grapples with racism, police brutality, and activism after witnessing her Black friend's murder. Living in two different worlds, Starr struggles to know how and where she can take a stand. In 2018, the book was made into a wildly successful movie, propelling Starr and Angie Thomas into more homes and minds. What I find even more compelling than the novel itself is the story of Angie, the author, as a child. It is a READ3 story that pulls us through Thomas's revelation—born of a personal tragedy—into her own explorations, then actions, which were followed by discoveries, dreams, and ultimately her book—Angie's own Declaration of Interdependence.

At a speech to booksellers in 2018, Dave and I were in the front row as Angie described how powerful it was to help developing people deal with crisis by reliving her own. Angie was funny, unassuming, pleased, and showing off some really fun shoes she'd gotten for the appearance. Her presence was genuine and inviting. She opened up about her life in Mississippi and recounted the most powerful of stories, intending to underscore how important the audience of booksellers and librarians is in lives like hers.

Angie described witnessing a murder on a playground as a child. Scared, not

knowing how to act, she got on her bike and rode and rode until stopping at MLK Boulevard. Her mother found her there, put Angie and her bike in the car, and drove her to the library.

At the library, Angie's crisis-embracing, determined mom took her trembling child to the librarian and told her that her child had just witnessed something that no child ever should. And while she couldn't put her on a plane or whisk her away, she asked for the librarian's help. She wanted her daughter to know that the world was bigger than the one she had just witnessed. She wanted her to know that the world was filled with possibilities beyond those Angie had seen that day and known thus far in her life. And she wanted the librarian to help her little girl find those possibilities.

The librarian took Angie by the hand and led her to worlds that were different than that Mississippi playground in the voices of wise people from all sorts of perspectives. And in reading those books, Angie, like so many of us, found revelation and explorations, leading to actions, which led her to make declarations that started as discovery, then led to dreams, and culminated in *The Hate U Give*: a Declaration of Interdependence that is now a major motion picture, which inspired me.

She used her crisis as a pivotal point to move her forward productively. Seeing Thomas speak to booksellers, I was struck by the way this one woman was using her experience to spark dialogue and understanding as to the ways that we can use books in particular in processing and formulating our response to personal crisis.

This book may feel like a reaction to the present crisis in our country, but this book began two decades ago. We were going through crises then, too.

The volume is up now.

The time is ripe for our maturation as a nation.

As I write this book, we are experiencing shared crises—plural—as a country. My work on this book began two decades ago, and we were going through crises then, too. But it seems like things have changed in the past couple of years. The volume has been turned up, if you will. Our shared crises have been amplified. How moving it is during this time to watch so many flock to their libraries and bookstores, professors, and churches for the answers, comfort, and guidance of thousands of voices and thinkers who came before.

Maturational development will happen, and we can do it well and with intention. It's sort of like Angie Thomas on her bike, peddling to MLK Boulevard, which she knew was her boundary. But chosen development will take us where we need to be—far beyond known boundaries. Chosen development will help us become, as a country, much bigger and better than any of us could imagine alone.

Chosen development will help us frame what we can do with the terrible things, the fearful things, the fabulous things, and the hopeful things in our worlds.

Everyone can do it.

It starts with something as easy as reading. Like you're doing right now.

Chapter 10

READ3: R Is for Revelation
(with Help from Reading)

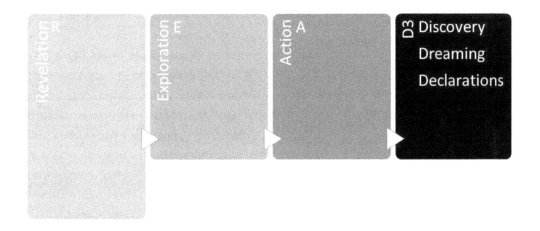

JUNE IN TENNESSEE makes me think of lightning bugs. I remember Grandaddy punching holes in the top of a Mason jar so that I could capture them and make a little lantern. I was in awe, amazed that those tiny bugs made actual light. It was an early, simple moment of revelation. An early "lightbulb" moment.

And while lightbulbs are an image we associate with the idea of revelation, I can think of more sounds than images to associate with the experience. There's the "Eureka!" The "Aha!" The "Ooh…ahh…" The yelp, the wail, the sob, the scream. There's the sudden intake of breath, the giant exhale, the shriek of surprised delight.

Try This: Writing Your Revelations

With a trusted other or group, consider sharing your revelational moments, big and small.

It's important to keep the words limited—condensed—so that their power is retained in brevity.

Examples:
1. "I realized I didn't have to stay in that situation—that I had a choice."
2. "I understood that my life had been based on an idea that was not true."
3. "I realized how much I am loved."
4. "A lightbulb for me—I needed to vote and participate."
5. "I realized I could do things differently than my family."

Starting with a revelation—sharing that important shift—can help you explore together.

Attend with care: our revelations are tender, private spaces inside us.

There's the quiet in the still of night that comes in a resolute sigh or a pondering "Hmmm." There's the hustling urgency of new awareness or the shuffling defeat of fatigue. There's the giggle, the laugh, the guffaw of sudden illumination. The snort of disgust. Then there's the loudest sound of all: complete silence.

Revelation has as many sounds as a summer night in Tennessee.

At something happy or horrendous, we find our eyes getting big. We've got to take in this thing. We've got to make some brain space, literally, for a new idea or way of thinking. We sit and stare, we get headaches, we take a nap or a walk or a run. We have lunch with a friend, we write it down, or we talk it out to ourselves. This is the experience of revelation. Of growth.

It can be as simple as getting a new phone and discovering its superpowers or getting a new tool and declaring "This changes everything." Anytime we make a serendipitous or on-purpose discovery and we have that wide-eyed physical response as we take it in, we're getting a glimpse of revelation's power. Did I really just see that? Hear that? Experience that?

A lot of our revelations come simply through life and living. We don't have to go out of our way for them. But life is an uneven landscape for revelation. The pressure to understand in the moment does not yield our best decisions on where to put and what to do with those revelations. The better ones come more thoughtfully, with paced exposures.

The very best exposures often enter through reading, where we go places we

Let Your Bookshelf Talk to You

A quick individual exercise you could bring into a group conversation.

Take a look at your bookshelf or shelves. What fifteen titles jump out at you? Think about what they literally say. Do they speak to a truth or fear that you have? A deep desire? If someone were to understand your deepest thoughts simply by reading the titles on your shelf, what would they know about you?

The words we bring into our world and the titles we choose can easily be read as a narrative to our internal, ongoing mental movie. We can often glimpse what our minds are working on just by reading the titles that we have chosen.

The same thing is true in a playlist of music you create or even the social media on which you click. Listen to your own words and see what they tell you about you.

the book, Jennifer recalls her head reeling with the idea that her life experience was not a universal experience. Others were truly different. Jennifer is an engineer—a highly intelligent person. But this particular moment was stunning to her, breaking open the cocoon of mental childhood.

Dave recalls the opposite experience. Feeling unique and separated from most people during his formative years, he recalls a revelatory moment that came through counseling in which he absorbed, finally, that his experiences were in many ways universal, not unique to him. He found solace, hope, and encouragement in the notion that his struggles were in many ways quite common.

"You're in me and I'm in you, and you can't undo that." My stepdaughter Jessica gave me that revelatory moment. After accepting with sorrow that I'd never give birth or adopt or be called "Mom," I'd been blessed with such surprising joy and so many gifts in the precious role of "stepmom." I grieved losing that place—and much of myself—in divorce. So, it was the most wonderful revelation to grasp that she and others in my adopted family viewed our bonds as unbreakable. It grounded me. Adoption is forever and cannot be undone. And what we have adopted in our hearts will continue. We are family. That revelation opened my mind and heart to gently, courageously, and continually exploring what it means to love and to be family. Chosen. Beautiful. Real. And always evolving.

cannot otherwise go and meet people we cannot otherwise meet. We listen best when we read. When we talk with live humans, we are often formulating what we will say next instead of really listening. But when we read, we suspend that dialogue and just take it in. We are open in ways that we usually aren't when we read, which is why it can feel like such a betrayal to read something written with hurtful or damaging intent.

My friend Jennifer remembers clearly when revelation happened for her. She was reading Pearl S. Buck's *The Good Earth*,[54] where Buck takes the reader through the life experience of a Chinese farmer with immense dependence on the land. Lying in bed that night after finishing

Think about your moment(s) of revelation. Where have you recognized that your interpretations of yourself and of your world were in need of revision? Can you think of a space and time where your ways of knowing started to shift? (We're thinking of mental changes, not physical ones, here.) It could have been a spiritual experience, a life moment, falling in love, a tragedy. All of these things have the power to bring revelation that will change and shape us. What are some of yours?

The revelations that really get in deep and have the biggest transformative powers often have to be absorbed in layers. We can't take them all at once because they require a lot of adjustments. These revelations often require that we change every layer of ourselves. Like a new page-numbering system in a book that's been printed, it's an effort to undertake. Sometimes our revelations mean that we throw out the whole book we said defined us and start again.

Profound revelations usually lead to an assault of questions, like, "How do I decide what I know?" If we're lucky, and we're doing the work, revelations generally play a part in answering these.

From the gentlest of changes to the deepest, the business of revelation is also the business of reading. And the beauty of reading is that the revelations slip in on the side softly. We can pick them up, put them down, and pick them up again. We can reread that book, article, or memory. Repeat that idea. We can see the idea in a context that is not our own and apply it to ourselves. Like a piece of chicken, we can take in the meat that we want to read and throw the bones over our shoulders.

Revelation and Dissonance

Let's talk a bit more about this dissonance thing. You've heard and seen and felt dissonance all your life. It's a chord or note that grates on you, a set of behaviors you don't see because they don't fit, that life element hidden in plain sight, or that niggling sensation that there is more to know.

The brain has an incredible capacity to filter and prevent us from seeing in new ways. And though that filter gets in our way when we're growing, it also helps us pace the growth. The inability to filter is part of the condition of schizophrenia—too many signals, too much information all bombarding the brain at the same time. The same mechanisms that help a newborn sleep through a crowd of roaring people or the noise of traffic are the very mechanisms that we must stretch in order to grow.

Have you ever laughed about the lyrics to a song you loved but misheard? Or learned the lyrics to a song you enjoyed repeatedly only to find in retrospect that you were belting words that boldly declared the state of your life while you were blithely unaware? We have a way of protecting ourselves from messages we're not ready to acknowledge. We keep secrets from ourselves sometimes: truths we're not ready to let see the light of day, because if they did, we'd have to deal with them and make changes we aren't ready to make. It is a common (and sometimes hysterical) thing to go back to lyrics you've misheard and connect them with a period in your life. Those lyrics can tell you things that others may have easily discerned about you, while you were blissfully unaware.

Try This: Naming Our Dissonance

In order to get at our own revelations, dissonance is a doorway and gratitude a gate.

Dissonance has many forms and names: discord, discomfort, frustration, confusion, fear, or even pain.

Since we can only work on the things that we see, it is important to try to unearth and examine our dissonance.

Here's how you can start letting yours lead you:

With a partner, name one thing that is dissonant for you right this minute.

The partner should prompt "Anything else?" and make no other comment.

Keep adding to your "dissonance detail." It is important that the partner make no comment and that you expect none. After each of your statements, the partner should prompt "Anything else?"

After about ten minutes of naming your dissonant things, try categorizing your dissonance as a single sentence: My dissonance seems to be about _____.

And leave that there. Trust that you will start unravelling this tangle just by naming it.

There is a worship song, "I Exalt Thee," that I thought for the longest time was, "I Exhaust Thee." I'm pretty sure that remains true.

Little bits of dissonance creep around the edges of our ways of knowing. It is a subtle little thing. At first, we might hear new language and experience the dissonance of the unfamiliar, explaining it all away. We might gloss over a term or expression the first, third, or fifth time it is used. But the seventh or ninth time we hear the word, we make mental space for it. It comes through exposure, and the very best exposure often enters through reading, where we go places we cannot otherwise go and meet people we cannot otherwise meet. Reading facilitates interiority—a space between just you and that book. No one commenting, no judgment, just a connection that you control completely. You can decide when to pick up the book and when to put it down, when to start the conversation and when to end it.

Like inadvertently rewriting the lyrics of songs, we often subconsciously (or consciously) choose books that speak to our most interior musings, those truths we let out to play only in dreams. A beautiful thing about reading is that we can creep up to what Joseph Campbell[55] calls our caves. Where we stumble, our treasure lies. Intuitively, we know that. The bits of dissonance that have been knocking on our subconscious are ready to be explored, so we pick up that book on an adjacent subject, creeping up on the thing that we fear in the cave. We know that when we go into that cave, as poet and theologian Pádraig Ó Tuama[56] has written, we may not die in it, but something else might. It is something that only you can discover and only by yourself. Reading is a pilgrimage, a chosen story that ultimately leads to you.

With that perspective, take a look at your bookshelf right now. What do the titles tell you?

We will miss what we're not ready to see. We may skim over a paragraph we don't understand, just like we may ignore a street sign that we don't expect to see or stereotype a whole set of people based on a single experience.

A group of people who have never seen blond hair could ignore the first blond-haired person they saw as an anomaly. The second, also an anomaly. Perhaps even the third and fourth. But eventually, the anomaly becomes a thing requiring the brain's attention. It requires a name, a re-sorting of the idea of hair color.

We have to build the framework of our thinking so that we can move to another level of comprehension and understanding. This is the scaffolding we talked about in the opening of the book. Until the structure is there, we have nothing on which to hang new thoughts. They flutter away like a paper on a windy day. It is possible to completely miss an elephant standing in the room if your brain has no place to put it.

How many times have you comforted a friend who was devastated to be caught off-guard by a reality that everyone seemed to see but them? What was clear to many who knew and loved them was invisible to them, despite abundant evidence that was compelling to others. Perhaps we ourselves have been that person, unable to see the proverbial elephant in the room until it is right on top of us and stepping down.

In our prayers and in our fears, in our beliefs and disbeliefs, we take journeys on the paths of revelation. Those journeys start with powerful acts of acceptance: "We are here." (The same "We are here" we've talked about for the country.) In his book *In the Shelter*, Ó Tuama recounts the story of a woman in New Guinea who returned to the area of her childhood, where there was no particular word for "hello." Instead, there was a word for "You are here." And the reply: "Yes, I am."

Revelation begins with understanding where we are, with accepting and leaning into dissonance.

In *In the Shelter*, Ó Tuama[57] teaches us how to greet our life without fear, or perhaps more aptly, to greet it with fear, and to find a way to say, "Here is what is happening." The kind of revelation that is powerful can only occur when we're able to tell the truth about what is happening, whether or not we think we are ready for that truth. It is a spiritual practice in this way.

Success in Circuit Lies: Seeking Revelation

We need revelation. And we need it repeatedly in our worlds.

When we look at the word *revelation*, we can see the root: *reveal*. Revelation is about revealing that which was hidden to us. It is about those mountain vistas and parenting discoveries. And it is about how we understand our relationships to each other, to the physical world, to the worlds we cannot touch, and to our faith.

Seeking revelation requires us to be brave. This is another reason why reading is such a good way to seek revelation. It gives us a way in if we want to

Try This... Quietly: Observation Exercise: The Revelation Quest

Recall Freud's idea that we often heavily display and pursue that which we feel we do not deeply understand or possess. Are you curious about exploring this?

Looking at this in our own lives is usually too hard, so we're going to start outside of you, in an easier thought space.

First, accept the idea that a revelation will always be a useful, good, deep truth, and full of life. Accept that our revelations are going to be greeted with gratitude because we understand that they lead to improvement. And respect that we see the revelations when we are ready, and no one else can rush that.

Challenge: The next time you go into the home of an acquaintance or new friend, notice the things and listen for the activities that dominate their life and space.

Reflect, and when the time and relationship is right, you can even ask, "I've noticed a theme. Can you tell me what is driving that?"

When you feel strong, ask a friend to do that for you.

swim but are fundamentally scared of the water. Reading can be paced wading or a deep-dive plunge—the reader gets to choose.

There's an idea by Sigmund Freud that seems particularly pertinent as we think about the imminent and emerging revelations in our lives:

We display outrageously and obsessively that which we do not fully possess or have deeply at our disposal.[58]

Sometimes our revelations don't quite have names until we have explored them a great deal. The revelation is such a fearsome thing that we cannot find a way to say it out loud, even to ourselves. Articulating these types of revelations can take years. Psychologists will debate whether or not we can speed the process, but if we want to get in touch with our present revelation and exploration quest, we can just look around at our lives for clues.

Here's an example from my life—a revelation eleven years in the making.

For over a decade, I spent most of my weekends and evenings filming or editing weddings and their corresponding love stories. In all, I edited well over four hundred full-length wedding films with the motto, "It's not done until we all agree it is done."

In retrospect, this is a great example of Freud's word *obsessively*. It can be our deeds as well as our possessions that are our revelation "tells." How we fill our time—rather than our spaces—can give us clues to the thing we are pursuing.

For these wedding film pieces, I recorded the family stories and love stories, interviewed the couple, gathered photos, and created footage of them together at their location of choice. For the wedding, I filmed from early morning until the last person left. Then I created a storyboard, finding the stories within the stories, as the counselor in me sought to be a mirror for this couple and for their family who would watch. Once, one of my clients' parents (both therapists) wrote, "You captured our deep dynamics and framed them in ways that gave us new eyes and hearts to see our whole family. This is beautiful—it is funny, healing, inspirational and aspirational not only for (the bride and groom) but it is a life gift—a gift of a lifetime—for our entire family." That was exactly what I wanted to do. People couldn't believe how much time I'd spend on these videos. I would work for hundreds of hours on each one, with a lot of sleepless nights.

I was always working with the backstory dynamics and trying to reframe those with musical narrations: Brandon, a groom, dancing with his developmentally delayed sister—making it her special moment, too, narrated by a song that gave them words the sister would listen to each night before bed for decades to come. Seeing tears from a bride as she watched and was able to see and receive the complicated love she had missed in her wealthy and absent father. Catching the rain on the red umbrella, reflecting the depressed and "lost" sister lagging behind the group and the way the loving bride stopped, turned back, and reached out to include her, valuing her in that moment.

To all of this work, I have only one response: "Why so much, so hard, and so obsessively?"

I had a full-time job and a half, a huge family, volunteer commitments—and this. I really couldn't afford to do it, but it served a deeper need in me. Many people video weddings and put together beautiful images in just a few hours, but I was trying to bring healing and new bonds, trying to frame this newly formed family. What was driving me to "outrageously and obsessively display" the world of weddings and family and marriage? There is always more going on in us than meets the eye, even our own.

It was beautiful to be invited to sculpt the love stories of these families and couples. But why was I doing it? I was obsessed with studying families I would never personally know and musically narrating lives and loves that had nothing to do with my own. What was the revelation I was exploring in more than nineteen thousand hours of editing and shooting wedding videos?

As Dave and I came together—after almost a decade of sorting through our own family love story—the deep compulsion to dive into those wedding stories vanished in me. Poof! It was gone. It's as though in the moment that we became the Uhriks, something foundational clicked into place.

Try This:
A Group Revelation Exercise

In a planned group meeting about this idea, identify a facilitator or leader and affirm that this is intended as a helpful, growth-oriented experience. The facilitator invites each person to share one of his or her "aha" moments in three sentences or less. Someone else in the group should repeat it back to demonstrate understanding (this is important). The repeating of the revelation will help exercise that muscle for each person.

Group Questions:
What happened and when? What was the dissonance that led to your revelation? How did that dissonance build in you? How long did the revelation take to be something you claimed as "knowing?" Did you consider this awareness a positive thing or something else?

As when I fell in love with Dave, revelations often come gradually, slipping into our hearts and minds with the stealth of what Emily Dickinson calls the "circuit." There are times when our truth—whether we embrace it as positive, negative, or spattered with both—must dazzle gradually.

Are you curious about yours? Look around your house. What is it that you display in abundance? We generally think it is what we love, and that is true, but it may also be a clue to the person you are becoming and to the revelation on which you are working. For me, it used to be clocks—everywhere, clocks. I've come to think that I was grappling on many levels with how I was using my time.

I walked into a friend's house and saw wedding photos in every corner—twenty in one room—and wondered, "Does this couple deeply grasp their own relationship?" They didn't. Another friend gets professional photos made of herself all of the time. Because of our friendship, I know she struggles deeply with self-esteem and suspect her exploration is about trying to be happy with the beautiful self she can't quite see.

Dave used to collect and surround himself with rocks from all over the world. I think, in an existential way, Dave was looking for his rock, his anchor. When he found it in us, the compulsion to collect rocks was like my wedding video edits. *Poof*—there was no longer a need to collect rocks.

Right now, I'm surrounded by books, and I think that is because I am wrestling with what it means to write.

Your environment and activities can show you your own revelations and give clues to the exploration that you are pursuing in the deepest ways. That's a wonderful, normal thing. That's what growth is about. And the more that we can grow with intention, the more we can embrace the gifts and opportunities we are given every day.

That thing you're struggling with, loving on, or obsessively displaying—that's the key to your most important growth right now.

As I've been referencing, one of my favorite poets, Emily Dickinson, sums up revelation in a beautiful way:

Tell all the truth but tell it slant —
Success in Circuit lies
Too bright for our infirm Delight
The Truth's superb surprise
As Lightning to the Children eased
With explanation kind
The Truth must dazzle gradually
Or every man be blind —[59]

That's perfect, isn't it? We can't individually or collectively get at our truths, the deep ones, all at once. We glimpse them in passing: a flash from the side, a dream at night, a fog through which we see a distant shore. "Success in circuit lies." We must go 'round and 'round a thing, a question, a niggling suspicion, a deep conviction, like a spiral drilling its way more deeply with each circuit.

As you read here, or in another book, pay attention to the things that unsettle or annoy you. Scratch at that dissonance if you dare. Or set it aside and let it ferment for a while.

"Too bright for our infirm Delight." The truth of love and life and freedom is much too bright for our humanity to absorb most of the time. Such developmental readiness comes as a muscle built to absorb, more. The surprise of truth is a superb thing in the end, though it may come like lightning and frighten us all.

When we were children, the truth dazzled like a lightning bug. But as the young-adult nation that we are becoming, the truth is more like lightning, isn't it? It is bold and disconnected from the roar of the thunder. Thunder is the information. I believe we are ready for it.

Sometimes, when we see that first flash of lightning in the distance, we grasp for a comforting explanation. We find ways to make the lightning less scary. We pretend that the storm is not coming. That is how we deal with dissonance, isn't it? We explain it away until the lightning and thunder connect and we must do something about all that rain.

So, if you're looking for on-purpose development for yourself and your community, reading for revelation, that's the start. Read and let the dissonance creep up on you, or seek it out bluntly. As you read, let the sounds of revelation reverberate in you. And then take them forward into the next step: exploration.

Chapter 11

READ3: E Is for Exploration

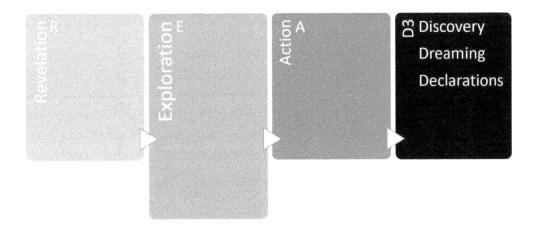

IF REVELATION IS the precursor to exploration, then we might think of there being three types of explorers, each stemming from a different sort of revelatory experience.

There are the Happy Explorers, who, with seeming serendipity, find a revelation that pleases them. Think of them like a happy Scotsman frolicking in a sea of flowers in a kilt. They'll make you smile. Next, there are the Purpose-Driven Explorers, determined to find those revelations and pursue the related explorations in an effort to better themselves and their worlds. Think of them like Sir David Attenborough looking for changes throughout our planet. These folks are

thinking big thoughts. Finally, there are the Unwitting Explorers: those who are afloat in a flood, caught off-guard by tragedy, trauma, or a big life change.

Try This: The Happy Explorer

Name one (or more) happy revelations you've had in your life thus far.

How did you explore that?

What did you do?

How did you feel when you were exploring this new revelation?

Examples:
- Falling in love
- Having a baby
- Getting a promotion or new job
- Buying or building a house
- Being able to go on a trip
- Being free of a constraint or negative thing

You know revelations and have had many in your lifetime. It's part of life and natural development. Here, we're breaking the process down a little so that your revelations can be unearthed or met with intentionality and a roadmap that begins here, with you as an explorer.

Revelations are just the beginning. The first step. In order for us to reap the full benefits and realize the potential of revelations, they must lead us to exploration. In exploration, we own the revelation, look at it, and set it across the room or dive in. Sometimes, the revelations do such a number on our hearts that it feels safer to begin in our heads, kind of running the perimeter, like a pup the first time he sees a vacuum cleaner or a cat the first time she meets a pup.

It's natural for explorations to begin in our minds.

Let's start with the Happy Explorers, those who come to revelations that please them, either through their own initiative or something more like serendipity. They are wide-eyed with wonder, ready to take it all in. Like a child standing before the entrance to Disney's Magic Kingdom, we can almost see the fireworks reflected on their upturned faces, slack-jawed and ready to gulp it all in.

This is us when we experience a revelation for which we feel ready. As a country, we can be that wide-eyed explorer, too—excited about new ideas, new technologies, or some miracle that saves lives or provides new insights or lets us communicate more effectively with loved ones. A new possibility is born, and we want to see all of the places it can take us.

To do that, we need to stop for a moment and mentally explore.

What does exploring a happy revelation look like? Well, the elevator has opened, and we're on a new floor of reality and need to look out from all sides to see what the world looks like with this integrated view. Revelations about technology are an easy place to see how this works. Think about the first time you understood that you could contact someone with your phone without talking to them. I remember the revelation of texting. It didn't make sense at first, and then as I explored it, tested it, thought about it, and tried little experiments, I found it transformative. It created a whole new form of communication that hadn't existed before. Texting gave a pause between sentences where we all could be more selective about our responses. It also took out the facial expressions and tones, so there was the need to learn a whole new form of language. I have a friendship that I've fostered for almost five years. She and I have never spoken, only texted. It's like a modern pen-pal relationship facilitated only through this medium—this revelation. Now, it's easy to forget that a time before texting ever existed.

This kind of exploring is easy—the fun stuff. It's the stuff that takes us into a museum or a new restaurant, that compels us to strike up a conversation with someone who is different from us. And they're important. These happy explorations expand our minds, hearts, and lives in countless ways. We're open to the actions, discoveries, dreams, and declarations these explorations produce because they feel good all the way through.

Sharon's Purpose-Driven Exploration: An Illustration

It was her brother-in-law's passion for his mission work that inspired her. As Sharon listened to him talk about his strategic approach to uniting those who were helping in Moldova, Sharon had a revelation: "I could do that sort of helping. I could offer something here."

From that idea, this educator quickly explored many questions: "Could I go to Moldova? What would the financial cost be? What would need to happen in my work and at home in order for me to do that? Am I physically ready for such an adventure? Is this about me or about the mission? Is this part of my purpose?"

After swirling questions, sometimes our answers come swiftly, and in this case, Sharon found her way to Moldova within two weeks of her revelation. As expected, it was life-changing. It created the ripples of discovery, dreams, and a Declaration of Interdependence that she's working on. But see how quickly we can move from revelation to exploring mentally to acts of service?

The second kind of explorer, the Purpose-Driven Explorer, is a bit more serious and intentional. From a societal perspective, purpose-driven exploration looks like us seeking out revelation, tackling big questions or concerns head-on to find out what they might reveal. Why am I here, and what is my purpose? Why does it seem that every society insists on having faces at the bottom of the well? How should education really work? How do we solve the problems of literacy?

At the individual level, purpose-driven exploration looks like the person enrolling in college or graduate school, or becoming intentional about learning in order to bring about a new sort of awareness. About a decade ago, Dave and I introduced a short-term peer mentoring process for adults looking to improve their job situations. There were 226 who ultimately participated, and I'd pose that there were at least three times that many revelations for the mentees and mentors combined.

Tyler Luellen was one of those mentees, and one of his revelations was that he could go to college. Just that: it was an option accessible to him. That profound revelation led to explorations about all of the particulars—not only how, when, and how much, but also where he would work and live, how his friends would feel, and what he would wear. His explorations gave birth to a dream of being a police officer and the knowledge that there were programs that would enable him to study and pay for college.

He had only seven short weeks of mentorship with his group of three students, but that time was sufficient to help him move away from living in a friend's garage (he was homeless). It helped him move away from a chaotic and unhealthy life situation and toward the pursuit of his dreams. He explored. He did the work.

Nine years later, on Christmas Day 2020, a van with explosives in downtown Nashville gave five police officers fifteen minutes to evacuate the area. The van blared that it would explode in fifteen minutes—please get away. Miraculously, those officers were able to evacuate everyone, and no one was killed by the massive blast. The next day, when I was standing in a grocery store, out of the corner of my eye, I saw the huge photo on the cover of *The Tennessean*. It was a photo of the officers—Christmas Day heroes.

And in that small group of officers stood Tyler—one of the five. Now, his face is painted on a building in downtown Nashville. He went from homeless to hero through a series of revelations that began with his courageous intention and the gift of a short-term focus from three college students.

The Purpose-Driven Explorer usually gets more than they bargained for—and

Try This:
The Purpose-Driven Explorer

Name one (or more) purpose-related revelation you've had in your life thus far.

How did you explore that?

What did you do?

How did you feel when you were exploring this new revelation?

Examples:

- Pursuing a mission to help someone
- Seeing a need in your community
- Wanting to educate yourself on a topic of importance to you and others
- Pursuing health in the face of a difficult diagnosis
- Trying to help a loved one
- Feeling a calling—a drive—to be involved with something

ultimately gives it back tenfold. And the power of the transformation is embedded in that reality.

As individuals, we are looking for answers to questions like how to be happier or how to live with more purpose, and we find our revelatory "aha" moments in the form of new virtues or ideas that appear to us in a book, lecture, or sermon. It follows that we have to explore those ideas a little. Which virtues will we use? How and where will we use them? In what areas of our lives should we make changes to have the biggest impacts on our happiness? Our marriage? Children? Families? Work? Exploring means trying on new things mentally before moving to action. We must see it in our minds before we can try it with our lives, and seeing it brings in the heart, as well. What we see and feel as we explore a new revelation helps shape the actions that will follow.

This brings us to the final type of explorer: the unwitting one. For the Unwitting Explorer, revelation comes in the form of a body slam—a wallop to the emotional and psychological centers. Divorce. Bankruptcy. The failure of a business. A cancer diagnosis. Being fired. Being offered an unexpected opportunity. Having a baby. Even finding love. We tend to think of body slams as the negative revelations. But unexpected changes that we view as massively positive can also feel that way. The Unwitting Explorer has had life yank one of the core cards out from the bottom of the house. Precept on precept, we stack our deck like cards placed end on end, and we live inside that

space. It represents all of our norms, our comfort, our stasis. But the Unwitting Explorer finds all the beliefs and theories once held dear tumbling onto the table in a pile. Where do we live now? How do we rebuild that house of beliefs and norms?

Collectively, we've experienced these moments. "We're not safe" was the revelation of September 11, 2001.[60] Since then, we've reeled from additional acts of terror and mass shootings. From this painful dissonance, we have been thrust into explorations.

COVID-19. Atrocities of justice. These revelatory crises ask that we rethink everything, from how we get groceries to what we understand about the different experiences, even life threats, our friends and neighbors regularly face.

The Unwitting Explorer often starts with protest. This can take the form of an individual protest (resistance to an idea or a need) or a more literal group one, taking to the streets to voice our dissent. We protest quietly or loudly because we begin explorations in a place of shock, then we get angry, and then we may reject the idea entirely. Eventually, we come to acceptance and ultimately a new hope. Those familiar with Elisabeth Kübler-Ross's Five Stages of Grief[61] may recognize the terms for the long-regarded SARAH model[62] of loss here. For the Unwitting Explorer body-slammed by revelation, this grief model is an appropriate one, even if the exploration is not about disaster but divine opportunities.

The path of the Unwitting Explorer often involves a certain amount of distress.

Understanding this process and looking to the examples of others who have come through their own traumatic revelations can give us the strength to do the same. Here, once again, books help us in both the literal reading process and the READ3 Model. Books offer the Unwitting Explorer a moment of interiority—a safe space between book and individual to explore new ideas and see new possibilities. Just as a text message doesn't demand an immediate answer (at least from me—ha!), a book doesn't require a response, so all the brain space can shift into absorption mode. A book is a space and time capsule for you—a study closet where you find morsels of insights delivered to your level of appetite and ability to take them in.

One of the books that has had the most profound impact on me is Viktor Frankl's *Man's Search for Meaning*.[63] Frankl, an Austrian neurobiologist, psychiatrist, and Holocaust survivor, was a practicing doctor in Vienna when he was sent to Nazi concentration camps. Body-slammed into the space of an Unwitting Explorer, Frankl chose to explore the library in his head and heart to help him find his meaning in that unspeakable circumstance. As he explored his thoughts and his suddenly tiny world, he found a path to actions—mental, physical, spiritual, and emotional—that led to his book, a declaration that ripples in me today.

Are there positive windfalls that make us Unwitting Explorers? Absolutely—but we rarely see them as such at first. The idea of the surprise is something most resist. I know a man who won the lottery recently: a big one! You'd think that would make him an Unwitting Explorer of the happiest kind. Though he knew he should theoretically be happy, it took him a few months to sort through what it meant, and to this day, he continues his grocery-store job, where he enjoys talking with people over produce. He's still exploring what it means to win millions. He doesn't trust it, doesn't trust his advisors, and doesn't trust himself to know what to do with it. We're funny creatures.

Embracing Exploration

Exploration requires us to pay attention. You've arrived at a revelation—now notice things. Stop. Get quiet. Look around, eyes closed or open. What do you notice? This kind of noticing can take minutes or days. During the biggest life explorations, it may take years for us to fully comprehend the new ways of thinking we are being invited to and all of their ramifications.

Imagine a world where all you knew was black and white, and suddenly your mind comprehends color. That's what a developmental shift is. And with that shift in perception, everything you've ever seen has to be rethought, reconsidered, and reclassified in your brain. It's a lot of work.

All your work up to this point—the pushing through the weeds of dissonance to revelation, letting revelation take you on to exploration—has not been easy. It often requires deep shifts in developmental thinking. When describing transformative spiritual changes, people often talk about a period of difficulty, uncertainty, or even torment. A yearning or a thing they could not name. "Rebirth" is an apt word for these kinds of transformations. In many ways, they invite us to become a completely new creature.

It doesn't matter if our revelation was born of tragedy or joy. Exploration means sitting with and fully considering the meanings of that revelation, which often ripple outward like water in a pond when a stone is cast into it.

When I fell in love with Dave, it was a revelation that came gradually, sliding into my heart and mind with the stealth of Dickinson's circuit. It was truth that dazzled gradually, deeply. I remember the moment of revelation, sitting in a chair, my elbow on my desk: "I love him. We are. We have been. We will be." The actual words I eventually used came much, much later—elbow on desk, chin plopped in my palm, I blurted, "We're sunk." Dave laughed. "Yes. We are." Then he put the side of his hand on his desk, palm open, and invited me to do the same, about twelve inches apart. I did. "Feel that?" he asked. I did. Like a bolt. I looked down and expected some sort of visible current. Then we went back to work and spoke of other things, because that revelation—the gift of a lifetime—felt like a very inconvenient truth. The words spoken by ninety-three-year-old David Attenborough[64] about climate change could have been about us: "It's inevitable, so you'd better grapple with it and cope and be aware that not only is it inevitable, but it has always been inevitable, if you see what I mean."

Now, why would I compare something so wonderful to something so fearsome?

Because the wonderful is often wrapped in the fearsome, isn't it? And that's one of the points of the exploration required in the face of a new revelation. We have to grapple with the things that frighten us most.

When we're exploring a thing, even those shocking revelations we send to their rooms and put on lockdown, it serves to remember what Grandma always said: the truth will out. Our truth—that revelation—is coming out at some point. Friends come around and hear the proverbial wailing in the background and slamming of doors from the frustrated revelation sequestered in its room. They say, "Mmm, what's that noise?" And we say, "I hear nothing." They say, "Seriously, something big is happening here." And we say, "Nope. Nothing to see here."

Aren't most children sent to their rooms to give parents time to create a game plan? To organize their thoughts? Our mental revelations are the rebellious sort that require the same separation sometimes. We will bring them out when we're ready to deal with them.

We tend to memorialize life before a revelation as an easier time. Mainly, we do that because it *was* easier. We'd already broken that previous shell, felt the hurt, and learned to fly with new wings. It's natural to want to stay there. We resist being stretched again and feeling more hurt and discomfort. But we should remember this: that thing we found easier was, at one point, a new revelation itself. We've been moving in this way all our lives.

I've noticed that my response to a crisis I cannot ignore is to put my lab coat on, retreat behind analysis, and start to make comforting lists. So when Dave said, "I want to work with you the rest of my life," my inner Judi Dench got out a clipboard and started an interview. "How long are you planning to live?" I asked. "Tell me about your parents. How did they pass?" (You know, the usual enthusiastic response to such a statement. Ha!) I felt compelled to rethink my written life plan, from which I'd been navigating since I'd gotten it all down at age eleven. And maybe that—working together—could work and satisfy this truth and not disrupt the universe. The wonderfully divine joke is how my careful plan went up like confetti and settled into a big arrow connecting the two of us.

A good revelation often prompts a heightened awareness. This new awareness is there to let us notice things. If you've ever been in a car accident, you may have experienced this sensation of heightened awareness: everything slows way down. You notice and recall every detail as your brain shows you what it can do when it throws the whole force of its power at you.

People often recount tragedies over and over after the experience. It's another way of exploring. With each telling, the teller can understand the experience in a different way. Each repeat of the tragic life event is important. Often, these tellings are to new people each time. And telling our stories is our way of exploring the thing from a different perspective, because each person "lives" in different ways to us.

I think of wedding photography as one of the ways that we explore the revelation of marriage. Every nuanced detail is examined in photographs and videos for our study. We see the relationships of parents and children and explore the ways those are changing in that moment. We look at hand-holding, at the furtive and open glances shared, at the details of dress and grooming. We listen to the lyrics of music, narrating our explorations while we dance. We look at the grandparents, the family and friends. We need this exploration because a marriage, like any revelation, is a process of alteration. An altered family. An altered commitment. An altered sense of self.

We resist that idea of alteration, naturally. Often, we negotiate mentally and say out loud that our revelation will change nothing. Friendships will be the same. Love will look the same. Life will be the same. But it won't. It just can't.

Revelation is the kind of seeing that can't be unseen. Exploration is how we accept and understand both the realities and the possibilities in our new lives.

Exploration for Our Adolescent Nation

When I taught the capstone leadership program for graduating business majors at Tennessee Technological University, I always began the class in the same way. I'd tell the students that the goal of the class was to lead them to personal revelations about themselves as leaders. In order to facilitate that, we would use the talents and strengths of each person in the room.

As our first exercise, I gave the class the task of paired partner introductions: each person would find a partner, and their job was to learn three things about the partner—name, something they were looking forward to, and the reason they were in this class. Afterward, we would go around, and each person would introduce their partner to the class of fifty or so students who came from many life situations, backgrounds, and cultures. This was always a rich room in which to learn, in terms of the human leaders present.

As each student was introduced, I asked the class to repeat their name aloud. "Hello, Jane Johns." "Hello, Sam Nash." I think some students may have found this part of the exercise tedious. But I wanted them to not only hear the names of their classmates but to feel those names in their own mouths. Then, after all of the introductions, I asked the class to pull out a piece of paper (a surprisingly difficult request!) and write down the names of every person that they could recall. They got one point for each name—first and/or last. It was our first quiz. The point was simple: the point of exploring together in a classroom was to explore together in a physical space. And the first lesson: we cannot explore unless we take the time to be more interested than interesting. We need to lean in to explore, to notice things.

For an adolescent nation, being interested is a struggle. Our current revelations are mostly about our very interesting selves, our own formative identities. And until those egocentric needs are met, the pull of the mirror will be unshakable. We

take endless selfies not so much to show the world our smile, but to see it ourselves. No matter the topic, we continue to come back to the revelatory subject of greatest interest: "me." And we will do that until we're ready to move on.

Someone could say the word "pickles," and the egocentric adolescent in us would respond, "I've got an experience of pickles to share." It's unshakable. I know because I question whether I'm stuck there too. See? I just did it. It is practically impossible to defeat, but I'm working on it.

A gift is to find a fellow explorer who can help by listening without imposing their own experience. Imagine America listening to a world issue without responding, "We've had that, too," or "This is *our* problem right now." We're not ready to listen to others or really learn about others, but we may be getting there. Many of us are still at the selfie station, needing a mature nation or parts of our own maturing nation to listen and reflect.

Hank in Tennessee found an interdependent fellow explorer who helped him choose development in a short-term peer mentorship program. His experience illustrates the power that comes with inviting revelation and exploring that new idea:

Hank worked in a local manufacturing plant, wiring lights. He was in his mid-twenties at the time. His first revelation was that he could go to school and that he wanted to be an electrical engineer. He wanted to explore the possibilities of that profession. Hank was paired with a mentor, John. Together, they met for six weeks, one hour per week. Hank found an interested other willing to focus on just him. In his first meeting with John, Hank revealed that he wanted to develop confidence and that he wanted to learn to speak in public. But when he spoke, he stuttered badly and found himself shrinking into the background.

So, Hank and John explored together. They went to a Toastmasters meeting or two, where Hank spilled his drink on the leader and gave a stuttering talk on that experience. They went to the local university, where they sat on the quad and watched people walk by. Unbeknownst to anyone, John, the mentor, had also had speech difficulties involving a stutter. The young engineer—not trained in counseling or even particularly good at relating with people himself—asked Hank the perfect developmental-perspective questions. "What do you think that person is experiencing today?" "What do you think that person is interested in?" "What do you think that person is feeling?"

John was asking perspective-taking questions, which helped Hank move from Piaget's concrete operations, where everything is mostly literal and self-focused, to formal operations, where perspective-taking and abstraction are possible. In order to be an engineer, Hank would have to learn

to perspective-take—to see and consider the thoughts and experiences of others. Engineers must use abstraction so that they can also hold objects in their heads. These two things, perspective-taking and abstraction, are connected, and instinctively, John knew that.

In the ensuing short time he met with John, Hank was able to get into the perspectives of others; he worked hard at it. And as he worked on thinking about what others needed, he found that his stuttering also began to resolve. Just seven weeks after beginning the mentorship program, Hank gave a speech in front of a celebratory mentorship audience of seventy-five to a hundred members. In it, he spoke about his new way of talking to people. "I just think about what they might find interesting and why they are listening to me talk." Hank spoke without a stutter and revealed that his secret was thinking about others rather than about himself.

Hank went on to become an engineer, got his first girlfriend, and is now married with a family. And it all stemmed from his willingness to 1) seek revelation with intentional development and 2) explore that revelation by noticing things, a heightened awareness that in this case took him outside of himself to see others. Hank explored by being more interested than interesting, and therein, he discovered his growth actions.

There are so many ways to explore. Like Frankl, we can explore through mental reflection and writing, treading deeply into what we already know. Like Franklin, we can explore through a group of diverse friends gathered in a junto, book club, or improvement group. Like Dickinson, we can explore through poetry. We can pray, meditate, sit in silence, and absorb. We can write, read, reference the experience of others, listen, look, and climb. Like Hank, we can simply decide we want to be better. And we will meet our revelations and then hopefully give ourselves time and space for explorations as we figure out what they mean to us and to our worlds.

Exploring with purpose helps us understand the breadth and depth of our new knowings, whatever they may be. And all that exploring, mentally and emotionally, ultimately—hopefully, necessarily—leads us to the next step of action. What will we do? When you've explored sufficiently, the answer will come.

As we develop as a nation, let's meet our revelatory moments as the important opportunities for exploration that they are. These revelations change everything. Before we leap into what they mean, we need to take the time to explore who and what the revelation affects and how. Let's notice things we didn't before. Let's remember that the good—memorializing yesterday's revelation as the "good old days" because we've gotten used to it that way—is the enemy of the best.

The Space to Explore

The vote was twelve to three in favor, but it needed to be unanimous. The back-porch revelatory idea that Dave had had about bringing jobs to Sparta had been taken to the city council, and three members of the group didn't want to explore the idea. One of the dissenters said, "We don't need another manufacturing plant here. We've got a new fast-food place coming." That was enough to shut the exploration down for the city council. The fast-food place came and went, but thankfully, Dave and I continued exploring in a different way, because we believe obstacles mark the path for everyone. Ultimately, thankfully, we found action, discovery, new dreams, and the new Declaration of Interdependence that is our little-big company.

This is one of the biggest challenges in our country today: finding the space to really explore a new idea. We've discussed that social media, with its reinforcing patterns and machinations, is not the safest-feeling place to hone a new idea. And we know that without exploration, it is doggone hard to decide what we think or know.

America has Happy Explorers, Purpose-Driven Explorers, and Unwitting Explorers today. And you are one of them.

Little by little, if we do as other individuals did—find our own ways to incubate ideas and explore revelations—we will move. Frankl developed, Franklin built, Dickinson influenced, and you and I have moved mountains, too. And when we move ourselves, we move our communities. Our communities move our states, and our states move our nation. We are pulled inextricably by a life that demands we keep up with those revelations and that we explore them. If we refuse the exploration, we will become a ghost of democratic passion with no remaining substance. But if we embrace today's revelations and their explorations—difficult though they are—we have the power to resolve the concerns we've been grappling with since we entered our American puberty about fifty years ago.

Think about the big questions then and the big questions now. Many remain the same. And perhaps you are someone who has been exploring one of those for a long time and you are ready to take action.

Let's be bold about our explorations, because we cannot become who we want to become—who we need to become—as a country unless we are brave enough to explore our deepest truths.

Chapter 12

READ3: A Is for Action

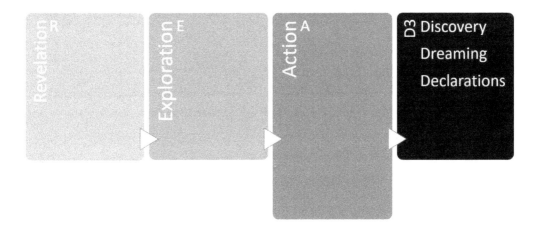

Revelation R | Exploration E | Action A | D3 Discovery Dreaming Declarations

I T MAKES A lot of sense that the Peace Corps and the space program formed around the same time in our history. Action—particularly service action—is core to our development, and these two initiatives illustrate the kind of side-to-side and up-and-down explorations talked about in the previous chapter. When we hit a new understanding—that revelation—we explore what it means on all sides (in the case of the Peace Corps, around the globe), and we're prompted to push the limits of our knowing farther, like the space program probing the edges of the known universe.

Born into privilege and burdened with health issues that facilitated the gift of avid reading, John F. Kennedy embraced many

of his life events for their revelatory gifts. As Alan Brinkley writes in *The Atlantic*,[65] "Historians tend to rate JFK as a good president, not a great one. But Americans consistently give him the highest approval rating of any president since Franklin D. Roosevelt. Why?"

The answer likely has a lot to do with the ways that JFK determined what he knew, how he dealt with life's most dissonant parts, and how he took revelations and explored them to the points of action, discovery, dreams, and the declarations of an interdependent nation.

Dave and I visited the Sixth Floor Museum[66] in Dallas this year while working with Interabang, a local independent bookstore. That building at Dealey Plaza was connected to books, too—it was the Texas School Book Depository. And it became known for a different kind of education when the president was killed by a shot fired from one of the windows there, stifling a potential that had seemed on the verge of aligning much for America.

If we're to take anything from our history, it seems important that we be selective about what kinds of things we want in our future. Today, I take his powerful words and intentions forward and respect the elegance with which he launched a drive for a bill that would end racial segregation. I appreciate his desire to provide healthcare to the elderly and poor.

Kennedy's revelations came from his studies through books and his travels and service as a young man. A family friend visiting him as a child remarked on the young JFK reading *The World Crisis* by Winston Churchill[67] during treatment at the Mayo Clinic. His big "aha" moments came through pain and personal suffering with his back, through observations and a deep lifelong desire to make a difference. "One man can make a difference," Kennedy said, "and every man should try."

"One man can make a difference, and every man should try."
—John F. Kennedy

A study of his life is an interesting look into how development works—how revelations led to explorations in thought, which led to paths of service action, which led to discoveries, dreams, and Declarations of Interdependence.

The ripples of service action such as those Kennedy promoted are still going. Decades after the Peace Corps started, I was mentored by someone who had been in that organization. It had changed my mentor's life, and it underscored the importance of service action in my own development.

Service Action Does Something Developmental in Our Brains

When my husband Dave and I FaceTime with our youngest granddaughter Lily (age one), she loves to offer things to us as though we can reach through the screen and take them. We pretend to do that and offer her something too. She also loves to wave, and we wave right back. What she's doing is part of a natural developmental process called "serve and return." We humans start service-learning as infants, and "serve and return" is one of the most essential experiences in shaping the architecture of the developing brain. The "serve and return" interaction between children and the significant adults in their lives is fundamental to the wiring of the brain from our earliest years.[69]

That same brain-building phenomenon continues as we grow and throughout our lives. Service-learning has long been regarded as a form of experiential education that supports deep learning. Through service-learning activities, students apply classroom knowledge in practical settings to enhance their understandings of concepts.

In the late 1990s, as a graduate student at Vanderbilt, I worked in the Peabody College of Education, where I co-managed a required service-learning practicum for all students in the HR and Organizational Development program. As I read their journals and rated their developmental progress for my researching professors, it was clear that service-learning was opening new ways of thinking for most of the students. I observed most experiencing discomfort with their current understandings of the world. I tagged written references to see how many times students referred back to themselves and the number of times students referred to the perspectives of others. Most of these students came from affluent backgrounds and tight, often narrow, social groups. But this particular program actively recruited athletes on scholarships, intentionally broadening the economic backgrounds of the student population. As the students worked exclusively in nonprofit settings for their practicum, transformational processes occurred. In their journals, students found the circumstances of the people they served in these programs unrelatable and incomprehensible. It was difficult for them to be self-referential ("Here's how I dealt with that when it happened in my world") when the problems were so foreign. Some protected their own worldviews with a set of psychological shades—seeing new people in new settings as anomalies. But others let the experience open their minds to the notion of wildly different life experiences and ways of making sense of things.

Closely studying the impact of service-learning over several semesters and groups, I formed a personal theory (shared by my professors) that service-learning and higher-order thinking are connected. In my own anecdotal experiments since, I've made more notes. Isn't it interesting how many people who act as servers in restaurants also pursue acting and drama? Yes, the hours often align, but I think it is more that the ability to get into another's perspective is essential to both good acting and good tips.

Babies, adolescents, and adults gain much through service-learning. At every age, traveling for ministry purposes is transformational. Our banker, Jerry Woods, lights up when he speaks of traveling, building roofs, repairing walls, and such in other countries. He reminds me of my brief time in Romania, where the dirt streets were filled with chickens and the water came from wells. I still recall being in a blind elderly woman's home in one of those towns. This lovely woman in a green headscarf offered me her only apple and asked me questions about faith and about my life. Decades later, I'm still stretching trying to get my mind around her life experience. This woman and her apple are still facilitating my growth.

Research on service-learning says that it improves problem-solving skills, personal efficacy, and understandings of identity, moral development, and spiritual growth. It also facilitates cultural understanding, increases feelings of social responsibility, and much more.[70]

Let's remember that revelation comes on the heels of dissonance. When you're uncomfortable, interested, piqued, frustrated, or confused, you're feeling dissonance. And if we embrace our revelation and explore it mentally, we notice things we didn't notice before. As we study photographs, texts, our surroundings, and people, energy for action builds. The explorations often yield countless discussions, diatribes, and deliberations. They serve as a sort of fuel that builds in us. That energy must go somewhere; it's a law of physics. Rather like a bunch of astronauts with a fire building below, we need some form of blast-off action, or it will not be pretty.

After revelation, after exploration, action must follow.

I believe this is why we get so very heated and passionate about things over which we have little direct influence. We've spooled and thought and explored and built this energy that needs an outlet. Training my Aussie puppy Millie at seven months has taught me a lot about giving energy an outlet: pay attention, throw a Frisbee, give her a job, or she will find one—destructively. When we see that sort of pent-up energy in our children, we get them on a trampoline or doing something productive around the house. When this sort of thought energy builds up in our collective America, we must move into action, or we will be like the astronauts on the rocket that doesn't leave the pad: both a waste of good thought and talent and a potential destructive disaster.

So here we have it: a continuum between explosive inaction and actions that can take us to the moon.

Let's circle back to Ben Franklin and his revelation in his early twenties. It occurred to him that he could set the framework for his own life. That's a pretty big revelation, especially at that age. This revelation led him to select thirteen virtues by which he wanted to live. He thought, read, talked, and wrote. In other words, he explored. Then he moved to action and formed one of the most powerful self-improvement models in history: his junto, a group of twelve diverse individuals without too much of a penchant for argument.

Franklin's self-improvement group thought about actions in their weekly meetings for forty-four years. When we envision this, we want to think of this leather-apron club having a pint and sitting about the tavern table, which they did. But the point of the whole junto, the thing that made this such a powerful tool, was that it was about facilitating personal and corporate action. *Doing something* with all these new thoughts and perspectives.

These folks weren't waiting on maturational development tasks, they were seeking more. They were looking for revelations, and looking to explore those revelations in diverse dialogue. But the real crunch in this effort was action. Every week, they reviewed a virtue and what they had done about that virtue, how things had worked out, and what needed modification and rethinking. Then they discussed a new virtue with two purposes: 1) identify an action that you, individually, can take to improve yourself, and 2) identify an action that you, individually, can take to improve your community. Action. Service action. By you.

As mentioned earlier, Franklin's group was pretty effective with their actions. The junto brought us the public library system and the volunteer fire department, among other things. We hold the same power in our hands today. Not only that, but we have more tools for connection and global impact than ever before, to do more and do things more quickly. We can take those personal revelations into a Franklin Circle or junto of our own. It doesn't have to be structured like Franklin's; it could as

> ## Let's Consider Dropping a Word for Our Wellbeing
>
> *Deserve*
> "Service," "serving," and "to serve" are all words associated with our growth. This word seems to be about the opposite.
>   Merriam-Webster gives us this meaning for the prefix "de":
>
> de-
> prefix
> Definition of *de-*
> 1a: do the opposite of—*de*activate
> b: reverse of—*de*-emphasis
> 2a: remove (a specified thing) from—*de*louse
> b: remove from (a specified thing)—*de*throne
>
> So could it be that our use of the word *deserve* is often literally about stopping our own acts of service and looking for something for ourselves?
>   When we think about what we deserve, we are in a headspace that is the opposite of gratitude and service. A gift or present no longer carries the same celebratory joy if it has become an expectation. Consider a mental check the next time you hear yourself use the word. It could be helpful.

easily be a book club. It could be a book club about this very book (what a great idea ☺)! However we do it, let's turn all of that exploratory energy into action that is productive not only for ourselves but for our communities.

We most often fail because we fail to actually do anything at all. When we take personal action, it builds understanding and strength and readiness for more action.

But the true gorgeousness of Franklin's model is that it involved thinking about service action, action for the community as a whole. This sort of thinking was the stretch—the developmental exercise—that enabled this group to be so influential and accomplish so much.

Isn't that beautiful?

Clean Fuel for Action

It would seem that Franklin's junto helped ensure clean fuel for action. By clean fuel, I mean action that is fueled out of a productive desire for positive change. That's an important concept: we need the kind of energy that flows into productive service action. Since most of our revelations come about through loss, pain, hurt, disappointment, or some other form of dissonance, and some people are in the habit of exploring things through the social media public rant, it follows that our energy moving into action could be volcanic-lava hot, leaving destruction everywhere those angry words and actions go.

Anger can come through thoughts or just arise in us like a lava wave. There is a biological imperative behind anger, but it's not really anger that we're feeling. Anger is a mask. What lies beneath that mask is most often pain and fear. We've seen it in the violence in our country—an unexplained mask of anger that is likely covering a world of hurt or fear.

Some people get angry like a tinder box and explode on impact, others are slow-burners that heat up with the passing of time, and still others appear to be cool customers but will experience a sudden eruption down the road. We need to acknowledge the presence of anger—not as a destination, but as the start of a journey. Anger can be an important and legitimate step during exploration. But the energy of anger is not a pure fuel for action. It's brewed out of hurt or fear and a murky substance. Anger energy burns hot and fast, with actions that don't necessarily produce any lasting change or positive outcome. We must get under the anger to the fear, to the hurt, to the root. And then we can move to the action—a service action—that leads to healing and discovery, new dreams, and ultimately those Declarations of Interdependence.

In the world of energy, we speak of things like sustainability and clean energy, harvested energy vs. wasted energy. Within ourselves, we can use the same terms. We want the sustainable kind of energy, the clean kind of energy, the energy that we can harvest and that wastes nothing that we've learned in our revelations and explorations.

One of my favorite verses in the Bible is Philippians 4:8, which talks about the way we think. I view it as a prescription for good health that I see echoed throughout literature in riffs and beautiful variations. The part of the text I like so much is about taking the noble, the good, the worthy, the good report, and dwelling (meditating, praying, thinking over and over again) on those things.

> Finally, brethren, whatever things are true, whatever things *are* noble, whatever things *are* just, whatever things *are* pure, whatever things *are* lovely, whatever things *are* of good report, if *there is* any virtue and if *there is* anything praiseworthy— meditate on these things.
> —Philippians 4:8 NKJ

The original text uses the word λογίζεσθε (logizomai) for "meditate" or "think." It's a verb connoting action, and it means "to reckon or consider." It shares a root with the English terms "logic" and "logical," or more properly, "compute" and "take into account," in the process of "reckoning" (coming to a bottom line) or coming to a logical conclusion. In other words, take the noble, just, pure, lovely, good-report, virtuous, and praiseworthy things to heart in order to decide.

"The noble, the pure, the lovely, the good reports, the true and the just." How much of our news feed has those things in it?

How do we decide what we think? How do we decide what to do? We can start with a respect for and regard for these things. We can think on these things as a first action, learning to adjust our thinking as something inexorably linked to our behavior and action.

Perhaps you've heard the phrase "simple but not easy." That's what this is like. Like trying to blow a bubble in the face of a floor fan, respect and regard for these is no easy task.

I'm working at it with the help of a really unusual alarm clock.

My clock sounds like a dog talking. Not barking, but talking. Actually, it *is* a real dog with a built-in timer that would be a watchmaker's envy. Puppy Millie speaks about my need to rise. I say "Shhh…ten more minutes." She returns to her bed then reapproaches in precisely ten minutes with more persuasion. Then I rise, tend to a few things, and begin the dogs' routines (we have four).

We live on a few acres adjacent to a wooded park facing the eastern mountains. I can't see a power line or another house, and I relish every moment of the sun's rise every day. For Millie (an Aussie) and Sweetie (a black lab mix), this is reading time. And like the most eager students, they race to get the scoop on what the deer, rabbits, groundhogs, mice, and other creatures have been up to. I throw the Frisbee and delight in the miracle of every in-air catch by Millie (who lost an eye at eight weeks). She's phenomenal. And as tired as I thought I was just moments before, their enthusiasm, the sun's promise behind the trees, and the crisp grass under my feet all breathe life into me. I say a prayer—often out loud and sometimes in song. And as I walk, I make a list—a litany—of things, people, actions, and news that I am grateful for. For me, it is especially important to be thankful for the difficult things—Dave's heart repair, Dad's cancer concerns, business challenges, our teammates, the sick, the

Try This: What We Feed Our Brains May Be Even More Important Than What We Feed Our Bodies

We are what we think in so many ways: the chemicals that flow through us, the thought patterns we learn.

Did you know it takes twenty-four hours for five minutes of negative thinking to leave your body? According to the National Science Foundation,[71] an average person has about 12,000 to 60,000 thoughts per day. Of those, 80% are negative and 95% are repetitive thoughts.

Where is our brain food? Like a diary of your food for good health, make one for your mental health.

What shows did you watch today? Were they positive, negative, violent, hopeful?

What media did you read? Did it give you positive, clean fuel? Or did it leave you feeling angry or repeating something you already knew?

What conversations did you have? Were they about ideas and building new things? Or were they about repeating negative experiences?

Guard your thought inputs like you guard your physical health. The two are closely related.

In her annoying insistence, Millie gives me something important, because I want good, clean energy for the day.

Thinking on the good things yields gratitude, and gratitude gives the best energy for action. Lately, Dave and I have been trying meditation in addition to prayer—just ten minutes a day at this point. It's a challenge. I make an organic veggie shake (always an adventure that makes me feel all proud that I'm being so healthy and good), and then we sit at the table, knees together and hands touching. (I can't believe I'm admitting that to you; it sounds corny. But we're sort of cheesy like that.) Using a meditation book, I recorded an audio, and we play that audio as a meditation guide. It felt really silly at first. We railed against it. Dave comes across like a tough Jersey/Philly guy who would never find himself in such a moment. I, too, thought it highly unlikely for me. But, convinced by research and a myriad of doctors at the Mayo and Cleveland Clinics, along with a good scoop of desperation about Dave's health, we decided to give it a go. And after three more months of procrastination, we did it. At first, I found that my mind raced with things to be done and problems to be solved. "When will this be over?" went through my mind. I used to fight that, but now I'm sort of embracing it and letting the words fly by. We both think that moment has a pretty important impact on our day. In fact, Dave doesn't like to begin the day without our prayer and meditation now.

We are far from meditation practitioners, but it is a small action of service

dying, those that need hope. Gratitude in the face of fear is like a good shower to me. It's a way of getting clean of the murk of my fears and concerns. And then I turn to all of the good things, the noble things, the cherished things, which is like a perfumed wardrobe for the day. Those who know me well know that I'd never ever have this treat without the interdependent, tenacious prompting of this hyped-up pup.

to each other (the shake, the prayer, the meditation) that is another way of giving ourselves fresh fuel for the day.

Watch your thoughts; they become words. Watch your words; they become actions. Watch your actions; they become habit. Watch your habits; they become character. Watch your character; it becomes your destiny.
—Lao Tzu[72]

Dave and I have adopted the image of trying to be like a kaleidoscope—something through which light flows, allowing all sorts of beautiful things to become visible. But like a palm set over the front of a kaleidoscope's glass, if we don't let the light in, none of the beauty is available to see. And how often I block that light! My fears, my pride, my silly notions that I can solve all puzzles—those all block the light. Sometimes, I find myself fearful that I will never be able to lose the weight I have tried so hard to lose, or that I won't make the right choices in helping others. I run around trying to do all the jobs and rob others of the chance to do theirs. I get in my own way so much! But I try to return to being thankful that I can move, grateful for the weight, appreciative of my health, and committed to good choices just for today (that's a tall enough order).

The morning walk is an effort to get out of my own way so that good things can flow. It's a practice. It's an action—a

service action for the dogs who love those outdoor stories, and one that serves and gives me the best stories of all.

Action as Productive Motion

When we think of action in our world today, we often think of protests. From my vantage point, it seems protests fit more with the step of exploration than action. It's a way of seeing who is interested and concerned about a given issue, who is talking about it, what we are saying and thinking. Protests are a call to action by the protesters. They are important, but they are only one step. The problem is, we sometimes struggle to go farther than that.

I have some friends who spent time during the 2020 election putting together an easy-to-read bio and collection of information on each candidate and promoting awareness of that information. It was a guide to all candidates, regardless of party, that helped the casual political person (or even the frustrated one who couldn't get local information through the barrage of national news) figure out who was who. But action doesn't have to be political or corporate. It could be suggesting lunch with a friend. Showing up to listen to a neighbor. It could be talking with a teacher and proposing a service for their classroom that you could personally do.

How often do we mistake changing our Facebook profile picture or a hashtag as taking the place of true productive action? We mistake a public tirade or speech for a real act with the power to change things. I certainly get this. It feels good to take these small public stands. There's nothing like a "You tell it!" monologue with snaps all over the place. And sometimes, many times throughout history, well-timed speeches have changed things in important ways. But what is gained if I make the most informed points and "win" the argument at the family dinner table? What is advanced if I confront my childhood friend on Facebook and try to convince him that he is wrong? What is earned if I "call someone on it"—whatever "it" is? Will that person be compelled to take different actions? Perhaps, but in my experience, this is rare.

Talking loudly or yelling usually doesn't help us develop our revelations or expand our ways of thinking and living. I think sometimes, we are like the children who say, "Hey! Look at this!" and when we get the focus we asked for, we're not really prepared to do anything.

That's okay; it is normal and part of the process of exploration, especially for developmental adolescents. But we must turn those revelations and attendant explorations into productive motion.

Action Is Productive Motion:
Four Ways to Experience Service Action

Clean something, serve someone, build something, fix something. Like Franklin's public library or fire department, action is something that has a tangible value.

1. **Clean Something:** Our actions in cleaning and caring for ourselves, our possessions, and our world reflect our inner states and often help us work through a revelation. I recently had a revelation about my grandmother and her work with her community and students and business—the way she served others. I cleaned a silver tray that had been given to her and felt immediate insight reflected in the sheen. I thought of how she served others and how I wanted to do the same.

Whether weeding or clearing a shelf or desk space, cleaning is an action that helps us see things. And if we can take that cleaning into our workplaces and communities, nice things happen. Last March, a devastating tornado hit our town, and people came from miles away to help clean. The act of making something clean—together—is a profound thing. It can be large-scale or as simple as what two associates at work did this week: they took an hour and remodeled the breakroom—a lift for all.

2. **Serve Someone:** Our service actions are like the best developmental vitamins we can take. I previously mentioned my observation that there seems to be an interesting correlation between those who work in the service industry and higher-order thinking and perspective-taking. Teachers spend their days in the service of children and youths and still have amazing buckets of energy for other acts of service. No wonder they're so smart. Think of how often sports teams engage in community-service action. It's not just good PR or nice to do; it likely helps those players think differently.

The value of short-term service projects for youths and adults is something we feel and has been documented in virtually every society on the planet. And as mentioned, the developmental research I've participated in thus far has led to my own working hypothesis: Service action leads to greater levels of thinking, abilities to function on teams as empathetic and aware teammates, and abilities to think about things like our interdependence as a country.

3. **Build or Make Something:** Action through building and making is developmental in nature. From mud pies to the creative land of *Fortnite*, from the physical building of stairs and walls and spaces to the virtual building of business infrastructures, the things we build shape us. We remember the things we build. We cherish them, and they become part of us in many ways, even when we build the same thing over and over again. Making a meal has a developmental value for the maker. It stretches the mind, letting our revelations and explorations come into their own. Those who build homes as part of Habitat for Humanity speak of that experience for years.

A few years ago, as team-building exercises in our business, we'd select community projects like building lockers in a school or mulching a playground or even constructing park seating out of giant rocks. Each person took away such rich growth from those small events. Working in the bookstore industry, it's a wonderful thing to watch throngs of customers come out to help set the store up—to help build it—as a community asset. Building elevates us all.

4. **Fix Something:** A broken clock or glass, a wobbly table, a painting that is askew, even a relationship. The act of repair is a beautiful way of sorting out our revelations and explorations.

Sometimes, I get so passionate and zealous in my revelations and explorations (shocking, I know!) that I see a shut-down look in a dear friend's face. Ever have that feeling or awareness and want to just pull back all of the words like a retractable measuring tape? That happened to me recently during a conversation with a friend about freeing herself for travel with her husband, the thing she said she most wanted. I saw her expression, paused, and asked her what she was feeling. "I'm feeling criticized," she said. "How about challenged?" I countered. *Hmm... no dice.* She was angry (with a dollop of hurt under that mask). What do we do in those moments? We can defend or justify our actions, doubling down on our point of view (not usually the best door to go through). We can apologize (better). Or, we can go farther, and after the apology, we can take action to make things better. (This is the part that I often miss, and I suspect I'm not alone).

Dave and I were talking one evening about the fact that everyone has a reason behind their actions; everyone feels justified in what they do. But not everyone looks at the impact of their actions on others. No matter how well-intended or informed we are, we can have impacts we don't anticipate. This is where fixing things in our families, places of work, and large communities becomes important. The follow-up action behind the apology.

My friend Amy is a great mom who always taught her children to say "I'm sorry." She always followed this up with "Sorry helps." As in, sorry is a first step, but not the whole picture. It's an opening that makes room where we can take action. Sorry helps, but it doesn't complete the deal. Fixing the relationship requires action, and those actions are important for my learning and development as well as for my friendship. If we're bold enough to look at the hurt in which we've participated, we will see things about ourselves that help us move forward. We dislike conflict, but perhaps there is power when we frame our intention on the front end: "I want to strengthen our relationship and learn something useful about me. Let's talk about what happened." This is another way we learn, when we embrace dissonance and offer gratitude and hope.

Outside of our personal relationships, there are larger societal relationships where repair would pave the way for so very much. I've learned that time doesn't heal all things, especially when it comes to relationships. Time just marches on, and sometimes, those relationship ditches just grow wider with time. And then we pass those rifts from generation to generation. Sometimes, the closer people are—the more aligned—the more trouble a relatively small difference can make.

Of course, fixing tangible things is way easier than fixing broken relationship ties. Perhaps consider starting small and working your way up to the big things. And sometimes, it's easier to get at fixing a relationship by doing an act of fix-it service for someone. As the adage goes, actions speak louder than words.

Back to the Place We Started

When we're sorting out how to live our explored revelations fully, action is the place where real learning occurs. We solidify what we know when we *do*.

Often, our revelations and explorations lead us, as T.S. Eliot put it, back to the place we started.[73] Only this time, we are prepared to take new actions. That is a powerful place to be. Franklin's junto was successful not because those individuals were flying all over the world. (Indeed, travel took much longer back then!) They were successful because they were using their superpowers to see their own communities and world in different ways and then taking tangible action. They were doing something.

We solidify what we know when we do.

I often complete interviews for job candidates for our manufacturing business. I've always found work samples some of the best indicators of capabilities, and they often inspire a conversation about what a person has actually done. I gleaned more from listening to Matt describe making a new bedroom set for his daughter out of pallet wood than I would have if he had spent hours telling me what he thought about woodworking in general. In working with Matt, I can attest that the actions on display in his story—the careful measuring and planning, cutting, and building—are the same actions he brings to work every day. Actions speak.

Service-learning is practiced all over the world—and in this country's community and collegiate programs. It is invaluable as part of the developmental stretch, particularly when paired with a good "aha" revelation. And we don't just need this kind of thing once. We need it our whole lives.

We were designed to serve others. We were designed for action. The human body improves when we exercise it, and the human mind expands when we serve and take service-oriented action. Those actions lead us to our treasures—individually and collectively.

As Kennedy put it, "Ask not what your country can do for you, ask what you can do for your country."[68]

Because it is that which leads to discovery, dreams, and our Declarations of Interdependence.

Chapter 13

READ3: D Is for Discovery, Dreams, and Declarations (of Interdependence)

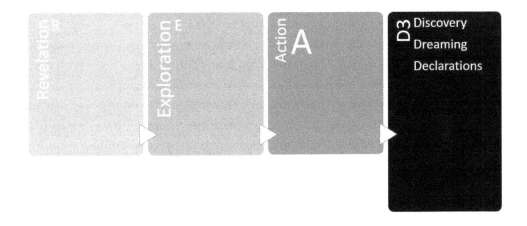

*D*ISCOVERY. LIKE A dazzling dawn, this word conjures for us something beautiful and inviting. That's the context we want to hold on to here, because in productive discovery, we find the way forward, a dream of a new possibility leading to a declaration about where

we're going and how we're going to get there.

Discovery is the joy we feel when the dirt reveals a glimmering stone. It's my husband's face when three of his avocado seeds sprout roots. It's hearing the voices of our son Dave Jr. and his wife Megan as

our granddaughter Lily pulls herself up for the first time in her crib. And it's Lily's delighted giggle.

Just like we remember the things we build, we remember the things we discover. Discoveries are uncovered, layer by layer, by our readiness to see and find them. They are often felt before they are seen.

After your revelation comes to you, after you've explored what it means in all the ripples of your world, after you've taken action that serves others and improves you, you're ready to reflect on your discoveries. When we have new discoveries, we can have new dreams. And those dreams become the foundations of our new declarations (of interdependence). Let me illustrate with an example.

When Dave and I first shared a home, my pretense of being clean and neat was quickly exposed. No matter my seeming level of effort, a parade of drink glasses followed me around the house, with multiples often appearing in some zones. Dave thought this a bit childish of me; I agreed. He was annoyed, and some tension ensued. Then we had a revelation: my around-the-house-glass-trail was not a purposeful slight on good housekeeping but a deeply embedded part of my personality that belies my organized upbringing. It's just that I get so absorbed (as I write at this moment, there are five glasses on my desk). This wasn't and isn't an excuse; I'm going to keep trying to change this. But it did mean this behavior was very difficult for me to change. I respectfully mentioned that Dave had different quirks that were difficult for him to change that I had lovingly embraced. And I proposed that every time I worked around one of his quirks, or every time he picked up one of my glasses, we might each view it as an act of love in action—an appreciated act of service. This was the revelation. We explored that, to our mutual delight. With every glass he gathers (there are many), he has a mantra of "I love her." It's turned into a good thing.

Dave is the definition of confident masculinity to me. (I have to say that to paint a complete picture of what I'm about to say next.) In continued exploration, Dave read a book recently called *How to Wash the Dishes* by Peter Miller. It is a small treatise that is accurately titled: it does, indeed, explore the simple act of washing the dishes and frames this simple act of service in a profound way. In exploring this simple revelation-in-a-book, Dave has discovered that he loves washing dishes. (Yes, I'm a lucky woman.) In fact, Dave's been thinking deeply about what it means to do this simple task. In the book, Miller writes, "You will know your state of mind when you wash the dishes: Your care or your impatience; your attention or your distraction. You will see yourself, at that moment, clearly."[74] Dave's now discovered that that idea applies to other simple tasks, and this has led to deeper thinking about what it means to live with daily gratitude for your partner. This, in turn, has brought about new Declarations of Interdependence between us: We've examined our strengths and structured the business and even personal things accordingly. In its simplest terms, Dave focuses on arranging the physical world, and I focus on strategies for the future. We both participate in both, but we lean on each other's strengths. It no longer feels like such a failure to me that I leave a trail of mess (neither is it something of which I'm proud). It feels like something I can work on with support. And he is exactly the right person to help me work on it, as I help him with his one or two *tiny* opportunities (wink).

This is admittedly a very simple example. But sometimes, our most profound learning comes from the simplest things. A simple story of revelation (seeing a bothersome thing differently) followed by exploration (adopting that new perspective in our activities of daily living) then action (an act of service, like picking up orphaned glasses or washing the dishes). All this leads to discovery—the idea that in these tasks comes a deep and abiding development of love. This discovery brings new dreams—a shared vision of our future as pillars in everything, from the smallest to the largest thing we can

imagine—and finally a Declaration of Interdependence. Dave arranges, navigates, and facilitates today and the next few months while I am freed to pull up and look at the next five years. We will determine our course together, leveraging each other's strengths.

The Effort of Discovery

A big part of what we eventually declare will be what we claim in our discovery effort.

Discovery is not always, or not even often, easy. When faced with something new, we are primed to see its flaws. But we cannot claim something if we see only its flaws. When we hyperfocus on flaws, we shut down the effort of discovery before it has begun. Thinking back to the *Atlantic* article mentioned in the first chapter—how transparency is hurting our congressional process—we recall that when ideas are immediately pummeled for their flaws, it is like a seedling sprout being met with scorching sun or torrential rains. Discovery cannot grow if we discard it before it is examined. An exciting discovery is likely to be rife with unanswered questions and obstacles that need to be overcome.

There's a discipline to meeting discovery that involves gratitude. Gratitude is not just about being appreciative of the easy. It's about embracing the hard stuff. It's about gratitude—in all things—with the belief that, as we embrace those discoveries, growth for our good awaits.

As a culture, it seems we are susceptible to the notion that being "blessed" means being free from difficulty. I'm not sure where we got this idea. "You're going to learn a lot, and this course will be a breeze," said no teacher ever. In the biblical Beatitudes, we see the word "blessed" used most often for those who struggle.

"The Beatitudes"[75]
Matthew 5:3-11

3 "Blessed are the poor in spirit,
for theirs is the kingdom of heaven.

4 Blessed are those who mourn,
for they will be comforted.

5 Blessed are the meek,
for they will inherit the earth.

6 Blessed are those who hunger and thirst
for righteousness, for they will be filled.

7 Blessed are the merciful,
for they will be shown mercy.

8 Blessed are the pure in heart,
for they will see God.

9 Blessed are the peacemakers,
for they will be called sons of God.

10 Blessed are those who are persecuted
because of righteousness,
for theirs is the kingdom of heaven.

11 Blessed are you when people insult you,
persecute you, and falsely say all kinds of
evil against you because of Me."

"#Blessed" is not only about a selfie with your beautiful family in front of your perfect house. It's about our moments of great trial, loss, and uncertainty. How powerful would it be if we could adopt saying that we're blessed with difficulty or challenge; that we're blessed in our mourning and conflict; that we're blessed when wronged? True joy is not circumstantial, and true blessings are found in our ability to use and transcend all of our circumstances.

Without a foundation in gratitude, there are no productive discoveries. It's like opening a gift and someone asking what you've received. You can say, "nothing much," or "something horrendous," or you can say, "something wonderful," or "something with a lot of potential." If we see life's gifts as useless, they will be. If we see the potential, we'll move with that discovery into something good. So much of our fate is determined not by what happens to us but by how we view and how we use what has happened.

Back in the 1990s, I used to do ropes events for team training with space-shuttle engineers in Palm Canyon, outside Palm Springs, California. We'd have these intellectuals of all ages do things like walk on a log or climb a pole collaboratively. (This was back before the days of weekend obstacle-course races, when we started doing those things as entertainment.) A strange thing happens when folks are out of their element and experiencing the fear of perceived risk. They are suddenly prone to all sorts of revelations about life, their team, and themselves. It was powerful to witness. In the shadows of the ancient palm trees, and with the help of good facilitators, these engineers explored their newfound understandings and tried out new actions and behaviors in the service of others.

Though there were plenty of dramatic high-ropes moments when fear rendered us all emotionally raw, looking back on my time doing this work, I am most struck by something I learned in a simple maze. It was during a program run by the more seasoned and skilled facilitators, and I was learning and co-facilitating the activity. The seasoned facilitators set up a large maze that had mud, brush, and a number of minor hazards, along with a clear and pretty simple path. We were told it would be an individual journey of discovery. We'd be going through alone. Did I mention we'd also be blindfolded? I made it through quickly but found it frightening to do it by myself. When I got out, watching my teammates struggle was more than I felt I could bear, so I donned my blindfold and returned to the maze. The facilitators let me. After about ten minutes of watching me help guide others, they called me out of the maze.

After all were out, the team circled for our debrief and described their experiences. One of the facilitators asked me what had made me return to the maze—to that individual experience. "I don't know," I said.

"But you do," challenged the facilitator. "What made you go back?"

"I wanted to help them," I said.

Next, the facilitator asked one of the participants I'd "helped" how that had felt. "I felt robbed," said the person I'd led out. "I felt robbed of my own opportunity to discover my way out."

It hit me like a wave, this realization that I'm so inclined to rush in and "help" that I often pull the wind out of the room and the struggle out of the person who needs to struggle. I was mortified. I was supposed to be an example of good facilitation, and instead, I had seen and learned deeply—discovered—that facilitation wasn't about doing it for someone, but about helping them do it for themselves. I'm thankful for that debrief and the discovery that resonates today, when I continue to struggle with the balance between presumptive "helping" (which is usually about me) and truly supporting the efforts of another.

Debriefs are not a modern idea. They were core to the self-improvement efforts of Ben Franklin and his junto: "What did you do? How did that work for you? What did you discover?" These reflections are core to the learning process, and yet, in our rush to the next thing, we often skip this rich, illuminating step.

It's important that we take the time to claim our discoveries, to write them down, to say them out loud. It takes practice and

Try This: Reading Books That Dream

One of the best things we glean from a good book is a whole new set of possibilities. Depending on your dreams, the list of books is going to be wildly different, but here are a few that speak to me:

Man's Search for Meaning, Viktor Frankl

Many Everests: An Inspiring Journey of Transforming Dreams Into Reality, Ravindra Kumar

Big Magic: Creative Living Beyond Fear, Elizabeth Gilbert

Finding Your Own North Star: Claiming the Life You Were Meant to Live, Martha Beck

It's Only Too Late If You Don't Start Now: How to Create Your Second Life at Any Age, Barbara Sher

Dream: Clarify And Create What You Want, Marcia Wieder

Check in with your local independent bookstore. The curators there are eager to help you navigate your own interests and the books that can help you dream your dreams.

a little rigor to take the time to own them deeply. But this is the sweet stuff. Let discoveries marinate, ruminate, and infiltrate your dreams.

And then dream.

Saying Our Dreams Out Loud

Has anyone ever pointed to a house you didn't think you could live in, a job you didn't think you could have, or an accomplishment you didn't think was possible for you? Has anyone ever offered you a dream? It's hard to even hear and credit these foreign thoughts: "I could live in that house. I could work in that job. I could run for office. I could go to school. I could live with a respectful partner."

Between discoveries—those products of revelation followed by exploration and action—and new declarations come dreams. Dreaming can be as simple as stating what it is that you desire:

- "I desire to treat others with dignity and respect regardless of their perspectives or culture."
- "I desire that our homeowner's association find a way to share the community pool and build friendships that would otherwise not happen."
- "I desire that we live together with peace and harmony regarding the daily chores."
- "I want to be physically fit and free to enjoy long bike rides together."

Those are little ones, but you know how to do the big ones, too.

Here are some of mine and Dave's:

- "We want to build talent in our community and impact literacy throughout the country."
- "We want to live to 111 and help build up eleven businesses that are independently owned by others."
- "We want to travel around the country, meeting our bookselling and library

friends and talking about how we can improve and heal our nation."

JFK dreamed of world peace and space travel. Angie Thomas dreamed of being a writer and influencer. Dave and I dream of being literacy ambassadors and helping our country find its way to interdependence. It is empowering to state your dreams. It feels big. Hard. Bold. There's a chorus of inner voices that must often be ignored in order to state them. You must shush the "You can't really say that out loud" sorts of whispers wagging their fingers at you.

We have an unfortunate level of comfort with stating what we do *not* like, what we do *not* want, and what we do *not* appreciate. The cheapest form of connection is the kind that occurs around a common enemy. It is a destructive spiral. We comment on a negative social media post with our own "hate that" message or become an instant ally with a perfect stranger when we share a glance of frustration over someone in front of us in line at the checkout. From Jesus in Jerusalem to the supermarket today, nothing unites like a common enemy.

But stating what we won't do, what we don't want, and what we dislike about a thing is ultimately an empty bag. If you went to the grocery store and only saw what you didn't like, didn't want, and wouldn't eat, you'd leave without groceries. If someone gave you a piece of land and all you could see were its flaws, and then you gathered a whole group of people around you who agreed with you that it

was simply awful, you'd build a whole lot of nothing. You'd gain nothing. You'd lose all opportunity.

But what if, instead, you had a revelation about that same flawed land—an "aha" idea? And what if you explored that idea, took action on it, made discoveries from those actions, and then let those discoveries turn into dreams? What if you could see something that wasn't there, something that you could create with this gift of land?

So why is it that we seem to find it so much easier to talk about and imagine what we do not want? In our families, in our faith communities, in our schools and our city council meetings, we constantly practice stating what we want to guard against, keep out, prevent, or discourage. I suspect this is a sort of mental and emotional armor for us.

A dream deferred is in all of us for different reasons. Poet Langston Hughes reminded us that our dreams, deferred, carry unpredictable weight and power.[76] In "Harlem,"[77] Hughes explores all the things that can happen in us—individually and collectively—when our dreams are set aside or tamped down. If our fears, limitations real and imagined, or pains and circumstances cause us to set aside our dreams, they can shrivel up, and our lives can grow tiny alongside them. When I see someone get worked up over something very small and inconsequential, I often imagine a shriveled dream in such a person.

When I see a person who seems to bark at every encounter or every obstacle or leave in disgust, I wonder: Do they have a dream that is festering like a sore, that makes them feel like running? Or a person who seems insincere, shallow, and materialistic: Do they have a dream that's crusted and sugared over like a syrupy sweet? Is someone who seems to drag and sag with the heaviest of weights in them dragged down by a dream yet to be claimed by the carrier? And when we look at an explosion—a shooting, an act of violence—are we seeing in that person a dream for their life that has been snuffed?

Dreams live in all of us. Our dreams are our truth, and, harkening once more to Grandma, the truth will out, one way or another. If we don't take responsibility for our dreams, we can end up feeling bitter and cynical, or we can end up afraid, isolated, or aggressive. Desires are planted in each of us, and if we fail to cultivate them, the consequences are within us.

Pause here for a second. Think about your desires. What seeds of desire have been planted in you? Be bold. Be courageous. Be simple in stating them. If you don't water this thing, it will dry up like the raisin in the sun that Langston Hughes describes. If we don't work with the desire, own it, and feed it, it will misbehave. Pray about your desire with gratitude. Meditate on it. If you are not all of you, who will be?

One evening not too long ago, I looked at Dave and said, "We're going to have to write a book about all we've been through these past five years. It is incredible to me." And he responded, "When has life ever been easy?" He was right. Life rarely presents a convenient spot for us to picnic with

our dreams. The struggles are real for all of us. We could argue who has it harder, but I suggest a different focal lens: looking at the very real struggles of others and how they got through them to open their dreams. This will do way more to build up our courage. If we look at those who are going through very real struggles through the lens of inspired action, it may in fact spark a dream in us.

Do we imagine that life is a conveyor belt that will one day deliver us the perfect sparkling gem of an opportunity? Like gems, dreams can feel precious and fragile. We want to protect them, and so we say them in whispers. But the brave folks who dare to speak their dreams inspire us all.

Let's be those people.

Let's practice saying our dreams out loud: our dreams for ourselves, our families, our communities. Let's speak our dreams that will transform today's crises—the ones that have everyone huddled around our tiniest of screens—into lasting victories.

Rewiring Our Brains for Positivity

Sometimes, I'm told I'm out of sync with the world for having dreams in the midst of grief and loss, disappointment and devastation. But it is precisely in these moments that I feel we have no luxury for the costs of anxiety and anger.

It takes our bodies twenty-four hours to rid themselves of the effects of five minutes of negative thinking. Let that sink in. A rant may feel good in the moment, but it releases things that you do not want or need in your body. Neuroscientists are now able to tell us that recounting a negative event or thought not only does nothing to alleviate distress, but also actually promotes depression.

Psychologist and Yale professor Susan Nolen-Hoeksema, PhD,[78] has demonstrated through her research how reliving a negative event is connected to depression, anxiety, post-traumatic stress disorder, and abuse of food and drink. And those negative thoughts conjure more negative thoughts, becoming a cycle. Nolen-Hoeksema's research has found that "when people ruminate while they are in depressed mood, they remember more negative things that happened to them in the past, they interpret situations in their current lives more negatively, and they are more hopeless about the future." It becomes a fast track to helplessness. "Specifically, it paralyzes your problem-solving skills," Nolen-Hoeksema tells us.[79] And just like positive passion tends to draw people, ruminating for an extended time frustrates loved ones, who may pull away support.

Nolen-Hoeksema, who's also the author of *Women Who Think Too Much: How to Break Free of Overthinking and Reclaim Your Life*,[80] says that women are more likely to ruminate than men, something that is possibly linked to women's developmental connection to relationships. As Nolen-Hoeksema observed, "Interpersonal relationships are great fuel for rumination," and ambiguities abound in relationships. If this sounds like you, regardless of your gender, I invite you to use

this as a moment to begin to examine that pattern in yourself.

Stopping the negative cycle is a tall order. Our brains are wired to focus on the negative—a fundamental instinct of self-protection. (Neuroscientist Rick Hanson has said that our brains are like "Velcro for negative experiences and Teflon for positive ones.")[81] The good news is that there has been a lot of research into the neuroscience of disrupting negative thinking.

Neuroscientist Donald Hebb had a revelatory idea about thirty years ago that is summarized in three words: "notice, shift, rewire." In Hebb's words, "neurons that fire together wire together."[82] He reminds us that our brains are not fixed, but malleable. The habits are not stone, but more like strong plastic, pliable enough to change if pressed to do so. We notice the negative thought, take it captive like grabbing a lightning bug from the night sky, and shift it to a more useful thought—our strengths, our opportunities for growth in this moment, the stretch and positive potential of the present. By taking in the negative stimulus and getting in the habit of redirecting our energy to solutions and the positive potential of the moment at hand, we actually rewire our brains for that response to the stimulus over time.

Hanson offers a similar formula. He recommends that we start by noticing the negative thought—fear, confusion, head spinning. Then we shift it to a moment of gratitude. We have to replace that negative thought with something different, and gratitude is such a beautiful balm to grab. (Remember: what is true, of good report, of virtue. These are the things we start tallying and computing.) Then you have the power to rewire your brain. It will take seconds. Think of the power! In just seconds, we can shift our normal response to negativity Teflon and positivity Velcro. By taking a few seconds to build stronger impressions and memories of the good things, the noble things, the things for which we are grateful, we are actually rerouting our own brains.

Sometimes, it seems we can shift to existing wiring that helps. Dave had a near-death experience that illustrates this well. In the way of boys, Dave grew up practicing jumping off of varying slopes of a barn in his Pennsylvania neighborhood. As the years passed, he learned to jump from increasingly high barn heights and even infused his jumps with a somersault or two. About thirty years later, while on a fishing trip with Dave Jr., fully loaded with a tackle box and multiple fishing reels, Dave slipped at the top of a cliff and fell. The fall was from about eighty feet up, with ledges along the way and dangerous shale amid the rocks at the bottom.

As he fell, his hands full, time slowed, and he saw the faces of the surprised rappelling people and his own leg rising over his head. In this sloweddown moment—as only our brains can magically do—Dave noticed what was happening: "I'm falling." And in that moment, he shifted the thought to, "I'm jumping." Immediately, the rewiring of his brain kicked in, and the training of his childhood came into play. He landed

and rolled from one ledge, dropped to another, to another, and then rolled to his final landing, stopping just in time at the lethal shale rock. After the adrenaline wore off, he was in a lot of pain with some cracked ribs, but his life was spared.

A day later, while trying to relax in a hot tub, he had a revelatory moment about his life. In that moment, he determined he would explore what it meant to live as though he would die in ten years. From that exploration, a series of actions followed that led to the discoveries, dreams, and declarations that have made what you're now reading possible.

I'm inspired by the idea that, if Dave could "notice, shift, rewire" in such a moment, this human capacity is available to all of us, if we seek it. In a very literal sense, his experience shows that we can "learn on the fly" and that our lives can not only continue but be transformed when we do.

What if we replaced all of the complaints, all of the rants, all of the ain't-it-awfuls and sympathetic nods with simply stating our desires? For my own part, I find this practice harder than any prayer or meditation, requiring the same kind of discipline and stamina that one needs to run a marathon. It's hard because, as previously mentioned, we're so wired for the negative. "If it bleeds, it leads" is the old news axiom. But it is critical that we stop retelling the bad news, ruminating on the sad, and imagining all that could go wrong, because this is the dream-killer stuff. The negativity and the fault-finding leads to those deferred dreams that will make us sick, sad, and lifeless. We are attracting health, happiness, and abundance—and the attraction starts in our minds.

In a 2006 documentary called *The Secret*, an assembly of writers, philosophers, and scientists share The Secret, which reputedly brought success to Plato, da Vinci, Einstein, and others. In alignment with all we've referenced here, multiple experts recount the power of stating the thing that they want to see. The documentary wraps a core nugget of gold truth in a sort of conspiratorial, whispered secret (unnecessarily dramatic, in my opinion). The truth is dramatic enough unadorned: this power of attraction and stating of desires permeates every major faith construct and spiritual discipline. The discipline they describe is exactly what Hanson and Hebb are talking about (and it also forms the core of Stephen Covey's 7 Habits). What these disciplines have in common is that they're all about stating the thing that we want to see—our dreams and desires.

"Love and gratitude can part seas, move mountains, and create miracles," we hear in *The Secret*, along with "Your thoughts become your life."[83] When cast as energy, all thoughts have power. Much has been written about the "Law of Attraction" and its power.[84] What emerges clearly, and is consistent with most forms of faith and neurological science, is that our thoughts have power. If we are to develop our dreams—dare our dreams—we need to shift our ways of thinking and speaking.

In the past few years, my incredible survivor husband has had several major strokes. Because he has displayed no impairment (in fact, he's experienced a sharpening of many things), it has been important to closely examine his situation via MRIs. To our mutual surprise and learning, you can't hide your life choices from your brain. If you're a worrier, if you smoke, if you drink too little water—you can see all of that on your brain. If the brain has been injured, you can timestamp the injury pretty closely. One of Dave's superpowers is learning, and as he has healed from these strokes, it has been amazing to watch him rewire his brain with intention. He'll say, "I need to go left, then right…" and find his exact meaning. Imagine our surprise when, reading a *National Geographic* article that showed detailed grid imaging of the brain, he exclaimed, "That's exactly what I've been describing! That's exactly how it feels!" If we didn't believe we hold the power to rewire our own thinking before, we certainly did after this. And the transformation for Dave has been powerful: he stopped smoking after decades, has a crisper recall of facts and figures than before, and has access to seemingly all of his memories more clearly than at any point in his life. In life as in blood type, Dave is "B Positive"—he works hard at harnessing those negative thoughts and transforming them. He is not always successful. But he loves learning and is confident that the brain can and will rewire. And for him, it absolutely has—not once, but four times.

We've covered a lot of ground in this chapter: the power of a dream to mobilize and inspire us and the risk of a dream deferred. We understand that we hold the power to defer our dreams, to sag and fester under their weight, or to feed our dreams by harnessing our thoughts and practicing claiming our desires. We know that negativity has effects on every system in our bodies, including our minds. And we know that ruminating, lingering in that negativity, is like hanging out in a toxic chamber.

If I were to put my goal of replacing the rants into Law-of-Attraction terms, I'd say, "I aspire to be able to get through a whole day stating only what I desire to see."

We understand that owning our dreams requires this intense positivity and a willingness to harness everything we have at our disposal—noticing, shifting, and rewiring on the fly, or as a discipline. And we know that we *do* have the power to rewire about our discoveries, to reframe our very thoughts in ways that are imprinted on our physical brains in the pursuit of our dreams.

Personally, I'm making a little progress on this, and it feels good. My dream is for you to take this book and these ideas and do something spectacular with them. Your big dreams matter.

Where they belong, and where we'll turn next, are our Declarations of Interdependence. It's a big topic, so even though it's part of the three Ds of the READ3 Model, it deserves its own chapter.

Chapter 14

Declarations (of Interdependence)

A S A CHILD and into my late teens, I was involved in National 4-H. I have still never milked a cow and remain pretty terrible at baking things, but I said the pledge, and I try to live it even today. It was an early Declaration of Interdependence.

It was a simple but profound thing, born of a beautiful model of continual personal and community growth—a model to inspire kids to *do*.

The 4-H program started around the beginning of the twentieth century with the work of several people throughout the United States who were concerned about the positive growth of young people. The seed of the 4-H concept of practical and experiential learning came from a desire to make public education more connected to rural life. Researchers at land-grant college experiment stations and the USDA saw that adults weren't readily accepting new agricultural discoveries, but that youth could "experiment" with these new ideas and share successes with adults. As a result, rural youth programs became a way to introduce new technology to adults (kind of like Apple's strategy much later). When Congress created the Cooperative Extension Service in the USDA in 1914, it included both boys and girls in these clubs, soon to be known as 4-H clubs.[85]

I pledge
my HEAD to clearer thinking,
my HEART to greater loyalty,
my HANDS to larger service, and
my HEALTH to better living, for my club,
my community, my country, and my world.

In the 1950s, 4-H expanded globally through exchange programs as well as nationally into urban areas. The organization's focus became the personal growth of the individual member, and life-skills development was built into projects, activities, and events to help youths become contributing, productive, self-directed members of society. By the 1960s, there was no gender or race division but a single integrated program.

In 4-H, we kept a record book for our projects. That hard green front and back were held together by an expandable metal binder, allowing it to get very large, and it was to be a constant companion in my life for a formative decade. We began every year by choosing projects with our facilitators. Those projects became the basis for revelations and explorations and actions that were recorded along with their related discoveries, all in the project record book. This is likely one of the reasons that I had a written life plan by the age of eleven. The record book prompted such visions and thoughts, grounded in evidence of service actions. A procrastinator to the extreme, I recall the rush each year to capture and record the actions and events of the previous year for competitions of all sorts. I competed in public speaking, dog training, citizenship, and even sewing and baking. The competitions gave me a feeling of accomplishment, and the record book had the effect of a growing resume, building confidence in the awkward little girl that I was. I could have success talking about Boxer dogs or teaching how to pack a good suitcase. And those successes shaped me

more than any of the other educational initiatives. The thing that held all of our diverse endeavors together was our declaration: a head devoted to clearer thinking, a heart to greater loyalty, hands to increasingly larger service, and health to better living. For whom? Not for myself. I am not even on the list! Better living for "my club, my community, my country, and my world." 4-H was a declaration of my interdependence.

I've encountered many models for growth in my years since being a young girl, when I was wrestling with my growing green record book with the odd typewriter fonts and sentences running off the page. But I have continued to think of this model, developed as a rural education extension, as a wonderfully sound one for learning. At a young age, it forced me to set a declaration of the things that I would tend to in order to offer something of substance to those in my immediate circle and recognize the ripples that would be felt around the globe.

This could have been a book about declarations, full stop. But interdependence is the key ingredient. Without an understanding of interdependence, we miss life, for life is an interdependent system. We have long hailed independence as the highest order of personal achievement, but that's just the middle ground achieved by a proverbial teen forming a sense of self. Interdependence is that space where we love, find relationships, nurture others, and understand how everything works together.

At this juncture in our development, when we individually and collectively are trying to move ourselves out of an adolescent nation and into a young-adult one, we need to be thinking about interdependence.

We've long been asking questions about our own identities. This is a necessary part of the climb, but the mountain isn't about discovering ourselves and being alone. It's about finding the ways in which we are connected. We know this deeply. In fact, if you listen, you'll hear references all day long. As Amazon's Alexa says, "We are connected." We've been saying it in the media: "We're in this together." We seek solidarity against racism and poverty, seek new solutions together for public health. We know this deep truth: It is not about you. It is not about me. It is about all of us.

Our Declarations of Interdependence are about how we do *us*.

To get your own juices flowing, here are some examples of short Declarations of Interdependence:

We are families that eat together, that celebrate each other's dreams and successes, and build and bind in the difficulties. We are couples that navigate the tight turns of self-employment and high hurdles of health challenges.

We are communities that collaborate and share resources when tornadoes or other natural disasters strike. We are builders of Habitat for Humanity homes. We support people in developing their skills and making life choices that help them live healthy, high-quality lives.

We are finding our common ground and having grace-filled conversations about our government and the policies that guide our country.

In our manufacturing business, Dave and I don't have an employee handbook stating what we do not want to see. We try to live the Law of Attraction and state only what we do want to see. As a senior professional in HR, I had been in a fair number of courtrooms defending terminations facilitated by the use of a thick handbook. When it came to our company, we wanted something better than that.

Here's our "handbook." It's a very short example of a Declaration of Interdependence:

We are an interdependent organization that depends on these four things from every individual.

1. We are ready for work: mentally, emotionally, physically, in the agreed timeframes.
2. We are safe together: watching out for each other and acting in safe ways ourselves.
3. We respect each other: we are more concerned with the respect we give than the respect we receive and offer it in word and deed, by what we do and what we choose not to do.
4. We give our best effort: every day is like the day after the interview—bringing our best thoughts and contributions.

That's it. Anything that is not in alignment with those four things needs to be realigned so that we can move forward together.

So, what does your Declaration of Interdependence look like today?

It doesn't need to be perfectly written, and in fact, you may want to grab a whole notebook or a blank Word document to give yourself space to unfurl your ideas. (Some people's Declarations of Interdependence even begin by starting a personal blog.)

Start by writing down your recent discoveries and your dreams. And if those don't flow, back up and write about your revelations and how you're exploring them and the actions that you are committed to taking week by week. When you've done sufficient action, the discoveries will flow. But they cannot come without the actions—especially actions in service of others. And the actions won't come without the explorations, and there's nothing to explore without the revelation. So, start where you are.

If you've got hold of a revelation, even a tough one, start reading about it, thinking about it, writing about it. A private diary means you're exploring.

If you've been exploring a new idea about your work and feel ready to move, take some actions in the service of others. Volunteer for a professional organization or nonprofit, serve on a board, or help someone in the field of your interest.

My friend Cindy Schueman had a revelation a few years ago about leadership in our community and the need for greater inclusion, greater connectedness. She wasn't sure what to do, so she talked and thought about it—a lot. Her explorations led her to service actions in several directions, with groups of people who would not ordinarily interact. Those actions led to her discoveries about our community's deficits and needs, which informed her dreams, which led to a Declaration of Interdependence with some community leaders, spelling out what she wanted to do. Subsequent to that, she received invitations from both major political parties and from an independent group focused on diversity and inclusion. Now, she is involved in creating more interdependent leadership in our community through a credible relationship with a highly diverse group of people. All of this unfolded in the last five years. It's pretty amazing seeing development at work.

If you have no revelations or are in the midst of forming one, that's okay. We've all been there. I recommend picking up a book or a few or many and read, read, read. Sneak up on your subconscious question. Let your bookstores, librarians, and well-read friends guide you. If you ask me, there are few simple pleasures more lovely than exploring the shelves of your local bookstore or library on your own and at your leisure. Let your mind trail the colors of the covers, light on the titles, and see what calls to you. Let the curations and the knowledge of the independent bookstore owner inspire you. Or read online. Find a new blog or listen to a new podcast. Reading uses more calories than watching a video or TV.[86] I don't understand the science of why that is, but I suspect it's rooted in the fact that when we hold a book and turn those pages—when we read—we're asking more of our brains than when we are absorbing a visual presentation. We've got to put together the pictures and the scenes and feel the characters from the descriptions. It's mental work—an exercise of greatest import.

One of the things you may want to read is our nation's Declaration of Independence, which is filled with interdependent concepts that we are just now, perhaps, ready to embrace in new ways. The founders themselves recognized their interdependence throughout their collaborations and contests and in the ways that they dedicated themselves to each other and to the people in those original colonies. They gave all they had not to claim their independence, but to declare that as a united, interdependent team, they were ready to chart a different course. The values of freedom, equality, and justice were written in broad ways with anticipated recalibrations. The very model of our government structure is a three-legged, interdependent structure through Congress, the Supreme Court, and the Executive Branch.

It's been a decade since my revelation—my personal "aha" that our nation is a developmental teen. And much of the time in between then and now has involved explorations, which led to service actions, which in turn informed my personal discoveries and dreams. And now, as I frame this message and its emphasis on interdependence, I find many voices starting to echo these interdependent themes. (Solomon[87] did say there was no new thing under the sun!) Dave Anderson wrote earlier this year in *The Hill*, "Although driven to secure both national independence and personal independence, the founders themselves understood that they, as Franklin said, 'must, indeed, all hang together or most assuredly we shall all hang separately.'[88] So, after 240

years, their kindred spirits would probably not object to our also having a Declaration of Interdependence."

These same themes are increasingly visible in the healthcare field, too. In a 2019 article for *Psychology Today*, David Strubler, PhD, writes:

Dr. William Glasser, the founder of reality therapy, places interdependent responsibility squarely in the center of good mental and emotional health. This approach demands that you examine how your behavior is interfering with your ability to form stronger relationships and figure out what kind of changes you can make in your behavior to get what you want out of life. You can learn how to reconnect with people from whom you have become disconnected and how to make new connections. If America and Americans want to be great, they have to be connected.

Strubler talks about dependence (on substances), codependence (on others), and independence (from others) as problematic. "If you find that you can't break free from isolation into connectedness—if you are stuck—get the professional help that can guide you toward interdependent health."

And, in alignment with our other examples, Strubler seems to have made his discoveries, dreams, and declarations on the heels of some strong service actions.

Try This:
Frame Your Own Declaration of Interdependence Now

The following pages offer a template for you to use in creating your own Declaration of Interdependence right now and a guided exercise for completing that template.

By writing your own personal manifesto, you will clarify your thoughts and intentions and align your internal world with your outer actions. Inner and outer alignment is the very definition of integrity and the foundation of character.

For the past [two] years, I have had the privilege of working with leaders in my birth city, Pontiac, Michigan, that was devastated in 1967 during the riots. We are making progress by co-creating a new workforce development program with Habitat for Humanity, the city and schools, Michigan Works, the Pontiac Promise Zone, three colleges (including my own), and the Greater Pontiac Community Coalition. It is one of the most challenging, rewarding, and important initiatives of which I have been apart. Some young people already have work experience and training and are gainfully connected and employed. Though we are just getting started, we realize that workforce development is an important cause around which even polarized groups can rally and contribute their support.

Strubler declares, "This is my Declaration of Interdependence—'that America and Americans can be both good and great as they mature into interdependence.' And it really 'doesn't get any better' than that."[89]

This is a good time for your declarations—the perfect time, in fact. In his new book *Enlightenment Now,* Harvard psychologist Steven Pinker[90] makes the case that not only are times not as bad as they appear, but we've in fact never had it quite so good. And he makes his arguments with data that prove it. Though I don't agree with all of Pinker's assertions, I do believe that the world is improving, and it can improve further if we embrace the right principles.

I've had colleagues assert that I am overly positive or that I ignore the difficult. (Perhaps not thinking about the fact that I remain the go-to mediator for problems that have gotten heated or out of hand.) I believe that the positive, *the possible*—which, for me, begins with the Divine—is where our rope is. That rope that gets us across those turbulent rivers of our time is a weave of the good, the noble, the true, the good report, and the virtuous—and it is a strong rope indeed.

So, there are the three Ds: Discovery, that set of "aha" moments we learn through, leads to Dreams, those deep desires that carry our keys to meaningful lives. Dreams lead to Declarations of Interdependence: how we will live those lives in health and connected well-being, working toward something better.

When you are ready, your own declarations will emerge, and you will appreciate the compass they will give to your life. Your declarations will need revision and honing, but writing down your own desires in the declarative mode will anchor you. And you will have answered your own questions: you will know how to decide what it is that you know.

Declaration of Interdependence

Drafted by:_____

On this _____ day of _____.

May it be known that my/our intent is to live and act in such a way that the following things are actualized in my/our familial and friend relationships, in my/our work together, and in my/our community and country:

Let it be known that I/we intend to live according to these chosen values:

My/Our head(s) will be devoted to…

My/Our heart(s) will be dedicated to…

My/Our hands will be dedicated to…

My/Our health will be…

For our _____, our _____, our _____, and our _____.

Try This:
How to Write Your Own
Declaration of
Interdependence

You're invited to write your personal manifesto.

As a person, a couple, a family, a life group, or a community, the time is ripe to create your own Declaration of Interdependence.

Let's break that down:

Declaration—a statement of intention, values, and beliefs.

Interdependence—an articulation of how you want to live and be in the world with others.

Interdependence can mean you and your love, family, community, church, nation, or world. It can be as small or as big as you're able and willing to make it.

Remember that first comes movement from dependence to independence—being able to care for yourself and move about the world independently. The next step, a higher order of thinking and living, is the recognition that interdependence is possible. It requires more of you—a collaborative posture with others. For the fiercely independent person, this may be a real struggle until the recognition dawns: interdependence is not about giving up your independence, but about linking your capabilities, efforts, and life to others in productive ways.

If you're interested in positively impacting your community and world, your document will outline that. This book hearkens to the original framers of our shared existence in this country and the Declaration of Independence. But there's an important characteristic of that declaration we often miss: interdependence.

As you think about your declaration, put up a large piece of paper or find a large whiteboard. Think big and perhaps start with your own version of Ben Franklin's key virtues. Then explore how you want to live those virtues out for yourself and others.

At minimum, this will be thought-provoking and its own brand of fun—enjoy yourself! And as you maximize the experience, give it the power to transform your whole world.

Chapter 15

Into Young Adulthood: Shaping the Next 240 Years

EVERY BLADE OF Tennessee grass was encased in ice, and the streets were no different. She had driven hours in that ice to a funeral in Baxter, Tennessee, because she wanted to give a tribute to her high school English teacher and counselor forty-seven years after her graduation. Marsha Cole had recently retired from a life dedicated to space exploration and science and wanted to give a tribute to the teacher who had inspired her, encouraged her, and insisted that she consider advanced studies and a professional life beyond her dreams. And here she was at the funeral of this ninety-three-year-old influencer. And she was not alone. There were throngs of former students in their forties, fifties, sixties, and seventies armed with stories of radically influenced life trajectories.

That teacher was my grandmother, Marie Swallows, and she beat the odds in Baxter, not only for herself, but for thousands of students who benefited from her belief and persistence. How remarkable that retired professionals would risk their safety and travel through the ice for the opportunity to share stories about their teacher half a century after their time with her.

Perhaps I needed to write this book because of her, at least in part. She saw the developmental need of a poor community with often poorer life choices and fed daily love, resources, and high expectations into it.

Moving our country forward into its adulthood can be a process that closely parallels what my grandmother did for her students. She began with reading, reading, always reading. She loved books and surrounded herself and her students with them. And reading led to revelation for those students. For Marsha Cole, it was the revelation that she could go to school at all, that there was a possibility for her beyond high school. And it was a revelation that she was smart and that career choices were open to her.

Revelation was followed by mental explorations. A good learning facilitator, Grandmother inspired with her questions: "How about this scholarship? That school? This test?" As her student, Marsha surveyed the options and opportunities, and new awareness was born in her. It wasn't just about the doing. Before the doing, there was the understanding, the revelation, the life-changing idea. Before there can be actions or dreams, we must take our revelations by the hand and survey the new planet on which we've landed. All the colors are changed. All the images are sideways. All the people, rearranged.

Marsha took her revelation about college and career and explored it with the help of one interested other. Isn't it amazing that it only takes one? The life Marsha had assumed for herself, with all its limits, was set aside as she stepped into the light of this revelatory idea. As she looked around, she found strength in the expectations and belief of her teacher.

From there, she took action, as development requires. These actions led her into college and papers and classes, where she had the space to dream. Her dreams took her into a new set of revelations and explorations, actions and dreams. And she became.

Our country can do that. Our country, one person and one community at a time, can read and be guided toward revelations that lead to explorations. In that new awareness—that new mental, spiritual, and emotional space—each person and community can take actions and cultivate dreams about what they will do, be, and have.

America, we are the high school students, and our teachers are the independent-bookstore owners, the librarians, the church leaders, the college professors, the museum curators. They stand ready to facilitate our development. We will experience new dialogue and create new community spaces where we listen and learn and broaden our perspectives. And out of those new perspectives, we'll have our own individual and national revelations.

We will find those safe spaces to decide how we know what we know. And in those spaces, we will find our "aha" moments— our most-needed revelations for these shared crises we face.

We've had them before. It was a revelation when we determined that we could toddle away from England and have a room of our own. It was a revelation when we decided that people could and should not be property, period. It was a revelation when we determined that women should be able to vote. It was a revelation when we realized that it was possible to explore space.

We've had a lot of revelations that led to explorations, actions, and dreams. We have developed from our nation's infancy toward this moment, where we stand tugging at our caps and gowns, ready for the national equivalent of high school graduation.

History has shown us that we have moved through the maturational stages of development, and here we stand, on the exciting cusp of our nation's adulthood. Now, we face choices. Who will we be?

The look on the face of a new graduate as she crosses the stage. A father holding his new baby girl. A young couple in front of their first home. The moment you say yes to the job. The new business owner holding the first check from a customer. That is the luminescent face of hope and faith, of overcoming, of victory. It's also the face of new responsibilities and of belief, challenge, and uncertainty. It is a beautiful face. It can be America's face in this moment. I truly believe this.

This is the moment when we plant the seed of a tree under which we know we will never sit. The moment when we become aware of ourselves as global citizens and, if we're wise young adults, look again at history for new lessons with fresh lenses.

This wide-seeing lens leads to questions: Where does this developmental awareness put us in comparison to more mature nations? What can we learn from their maturational journeys?

It's hard. Every person who falls in love for the first time is certain that theirs is the first true love. The only love. The one no one else has ever had an experience quite like. We feel unique, special, born for purpose. As lovely as that feeling is, there is a maturity beyond it that we must reach, and it comes with a humility of spirit, a willingness to look at our elders to see what we wish to keep.

We've been given so much, and as with a gifted piece of land, it is up to us not to

succumb to the habit of seeking the flaws of these gifts. It is up to us to shift the narrative from biting, destructive social posts to action that has real, and positive, traction going forward.

"Respect" comes from the Latin *respectus*—"re" and "spect." Literally, respect means the willingness to look (spect) again (re). "I respect you" communicates "I'm willing to look again at you, your idea, or your position." There is an old parable that illustrates respect and our need for it beautifully. The idea of the parable is that six men of Indostan (to learning much inclined) went to see an elephant (though all of them were blind), that each by observation might satisfy his mind. As the parable unfolds, they all land on this large being in different spots and declare their truth—the very definition of an elephant, courtesy of their individual (and limited) perspectives. One thinks the elephant a wall, having landed on its side. Another argues the elephant is like a spear, touching the tusk. The third, holding the trunk, thinks the elephant is more like a snake. The fourth, feeling about the knee, argues his case that the elephant is like a tree. The fifth scoffs, declaring the elephant is like a fan as he holds the ear. And the sixth, grabbing the tail, proclaims the elephant is like a rope (perhaps a smelly one).

Who is right and who is wrong? Everyone. And how will they ever figure out what this thing really is? It starts with receiving those different perspectives with gratitude and respect—looking again. If someone sees a metaphorical fan while you're finding a wall, that is really good news, because if you put your perspectives together, you can create a picture that is bigger than your own view. And we need those big perspectives—the gifts of each other's perspectives—to interdependently figure out what our big elephants in the room are really about.

Name your elephant: poverty, education, healthcare, discrimination, abuse, the struggle of a small business, or the needs of families in your community. In order to piece these things together, the sizes of the problems require that we work in interdependent ways and that we be more concerned about the respect we give others' perspectives than the respect we receive. Across our country today, from city councils to Senate hearings, proverbial elephants are debated. Your position on education needs will be different than thirty other people's positions on the same, because all of those positions likely stem from a limited but valuable perspective. What we need, in learning about how to work interdependently, is to learn how to piece together those perspectives like puzzle clues helping us see the whole of a thing. Instead of debate or discussion (a word sharing a root with "percussion," and literally meaning to beat ideas at each other like beating a drum), we need collaborative dialogue that builds. And that dialogue begins with respect—looking again at a perspective that seems really bizarre to you.

Will we look again? Will we heighten our awareness and take in more information? Can we look at each other with wide-eyed wonder and find the beautiful thing, the thing we appreciate and want to collaborate with? I hope so.

We have the benefit of a lot of history. We have at our fingertips, more than any generation before us, the opportunity to know more. We have the opportunity to see the connections—to find and foster interdependence in so many ways. We can break free of the algorithms that feed our daily thoughts by searching and asking questions, by reading outside of our self-reinforcing norms. And we must do that work if we're to discover the "elephants" that matter most to us now.

Such movement will not be easy. It will require that we choose development, which means leaping from what you know into a lot of unknown. It means running toward, not running away from, dissonance. It can mean letting go of everything you thought you knew before your fingers are able to grasp a new awareness, like a hand reaching out in the dark. In that new awareness, you may experience a profound feeling of alienation, because you've left behind all you were before.

If you're a learner who wants to grow, who wants to know and be more, then knowing that this option exists is irresistible. You'll have to pursue it. Reading can help you move through your developmental journey at your own pace. Book clubs, a junto like Franklin's circle, or other groups can help you find differentiation and connection as you define your own actions. And if you're the brave soul I believe you are, you'll pursue development, not just for yourself, but for the benefit of all you love.

We have just one planet to share. Your community needs you to become the kind of person who thinks at higher levels, the kind of person who can get away from the egocentric pull of the self and be available for others. The kind of person who can share the crises and build a better US.

The concrete in our country is wet. Let's move our collective energies from social-media rants and complaints toward a society that we want to live and participate in. What we feed grows. Let's be intentional about the gardens we're cultivating every day.

The harder the circumstance, the more important it is that every ounce of our life energy be directed at something better, finer, more full of grace.

As one of my favorite songs from the musical *Hamilton* says, "History has its eyes on you."[91] *We* are telling our own stories now. This is our moment—our time—to find our revelations, explore new ways, act in service, and expand our thinking so that we may discover new things, dream new dreams, and be framers of a reborn declaration, one that claims the whole of the originators' intent. A Declaration of *Inter*dependence. As the musical inspires, it is time for us to "look around, look around" at how wonderful it is to be alive right now, to be in a position to shape this moldable clay that is the Unites States. Let's take "our shot."

Dissonance is the doorway. Life has never been and will never be easy. And we greet our personal dissonance with gratitude, because gratitude is that great judo move, and it is in our owner's manual. Our systems fire on all cylinders when we grab the difficult and give it gratitude.

When we offer appreciative hearts for all that we encounter, we will grow, we will learn, and we will develop and actualize the dreams and visions planted in our cores. America is becoming—and with our intention and effort, we can move through our nation's adolescence into the country we have always wanted to be.

I conclude knowing that this book doesn't matter. My faith and prayers are with you, because what you do with the ideas in this book matters. Thank you for reading, thinking, and working to become the America in which we all want to live.

Companion Quotes for Group Topical Discussion

Interdependence

it is in the shelter of each other that the people live

ar scáth a chéile a mhaireas na daoine[92]

America Adulting

If we don't change, we don't grow. If we don't grow, we aren't really living.
—**Gail Sheehy**[93]

No matter how different the forms we choose, our concentration during the Trying Twenties is on mastering what we feel we are supposed to do.
—**Gail Sheehy,** *Passages:*
Predictable Crises of Adult Life[94]

Dissonance

Pain insists upon being attended to. God whispers to us in our pleasures, speaks in our consciences, but shouts in our pains. It is his megaphone to rouse a deaf world.
—**C. S. Lewis**[95]

Turn your wounds into wisdom.

—Oprah Winfrey[96]

It is frightening to step off onto the treacherous footbridge leading to the second half of life. We can't take everything with us on this journey through uncertainty. Along the way, we discover that we are alone. We no longer have to ask permission because we are the providers of our own safety. We must learn to give ourselves permission. We stumble upon feminine or masculine aspects of our natures that up to this time have usually been masked. There is grieving to be done because an old self is dying. By taking in our suppressed and even our unwanted parts, we prepare at the gut level for the reintegration of an identity that is ours and ours alone—not some artificial form put together to please the culture or our mates. It is a dark passage at the beginning. But by disassembling ourselves, we can glimpse the light and gather our parts into a renewal.

—Gail Sheehy,
Passages: Predictable Crises of Adult Life[97]

The deeper that sorrow carves into your being, the more joy you can contain.

Is not the cup that holds your wine the very cup that was burned in the potter's oven?

And is not the lute that soothes your spirit, the very wood that was hollowed with knives?

When you are joyous, look deep into your heart and you shall find it is only that which has given you sorrow that is giving you joy.

When you are sorrowful look again in your heart, and you shall see that in truth you are weeping for that which has been your delight.

—Kahlil Gibran[98]

You get to know who you really are in a crisis.

—Oprah Winfrey[99]

Out of suffering have emerged the strongest souls; the most massive characters are seared with scars.

—Kahlil Gibran[100]

Revelation

It takes courage...to endure the sharp pains of self discovery rather than choose to take the dull pain of unconsciousness that would last the rest of our lives.

—Marianne Williamson,
A Return to Love: Reflections on the Principles of "A Course in Miracles"[101]

The pessimist resembles a man who observes with fear and sadness that his wall calendar, from which he daily tears a sheet, grows thinner with each passing day. On the other hand, the person who attacks the problems of life actively is like a man who removes each successive leaf from his calendar and files it neatly and carefully away with its predecessors, after first having jotted down a few diary notes on the back. He can reflect with pride and joy on all the richness set down in these notes, on all the life he has already lived to the fullest. What will it matter to him if he notices that he is growing old? Has he any reason to envy the young people whom he sees, or wax nostalgic over his own lost youth? What reasons has he to envy a young person? For the possibilities that a young person has, the future which is in store for him?

"No, thank you," he will think. "Instead of possibilities, I have realities in my past, not only the reality of work done and of love loved, but of sufferings bravely suffered. These sufferings are even the things of which I am most proud, although these are things which cannot inspire envy."

—Viktor E. Frankl, *Man's Search for Meaning*[102]

Gratitude

I trust that everything happens for a reason, even if we are not wise enough to see it.

—Oprah Winfrey[103]

Piglet noticed that even though he had a Very Small Heart, it could hold a rather large amount of Gratitude.

—A. A. Milne, *Winnie-the-Pooh*[104]

You pray in your distress and in your need; would that you might pray also in the fullness of your joy and in your days of abundance.

—Kahlil Gibran, *The Prophet*[105]

What separates privilege from entitlement is gratitude.

—Brené Brown[106]

Whatever you appreciate and give thanks for will increase in your life.

—Sanaya Roman,
Living with Joy: Keys to Personal Power and Spiritual Transformation[107]

Let gratitude be the pillow upon which you kneel to say your nightly prayer. And let faith be the bridge you build to overcome evil and welcome good.

—Maya Angelou,
Celebrations: Rituals of Peace and Prayer[108]

Saying that "I am a grateful alcoholic" will then reflect the truth about who we have become in our person, having understood deeply and intimately that God in his grace can turn any evil, any pain we have suffered or inflicted, to good purpose.

—Ray A.,
Practice These Principles: Living the Spiritual Disciplines and Virtues in 12-Step Recovery to Achieve Spiritual Growth, Character Development, and Emotional Sobriety[109]

True gratitude is about the ordinary.

—Anthon St. Maarten[110]

Exploration

Perplexity is the beginning of knowledge.

—Kahlil Gibran[111]

One's own religion is after all a matter between oneself and one's Maker and no one else's.

—Kahlil Gibran[112]

Man cannot discover new oceans unless he has the courage to lose sight of the shore.

—André Gide[113]

In wisdom gathered over time I have found that every experience is a form of exploration.

—Ansel Adams[114]

A person does not grow from the ground like a vine or a tree, one is not part of a plot of land. Mankind has legs so it can wander.

—Roman Payne,
The Wanderess[115]

Before he goes into the water, a diver cannot know what he will bring back.

—Max Ernst[116]

The camera basically is a license to explore.

—**Jerry Uelsmann**[117]

Not all doors open in the same direction and with the same effort!

—**Jasleen Kaur Gumber**[118]

Only I can change my life. No one can do it for me.

—**Carol Burnett**[119]

Read more: https://www.spiritbutton.com/change-quotes/#ixzz6k311Go2k

Action in Service of Others

Each of us has a unique part to play in the healing of the world.

—**Marianne Williamson,**
The Law of Divine Compensation: On Work, Money, and Miracles[120]

Success means we go to sleep at night knowing that our talents and abilities were used in a way that served others.

—**Marianne Williamson**[121]

In every community, there is work to be done.
In every nation, there are wounds to heal.
In every heart, there is the power to do it.

—**Marianne Williamson**[122]

You give but little when you give of your possessions.
It is when you give of yourself that you truly give.

—**Kahlil Gibran,**
The Prophet[123]

How we spend our days is, of course, how we spend our lives.

—**Annie Dillard**[124]

Strengths and Notice, Shift, Rewire

Your true passion should feel like breathing; it's that natural.
—**Oprah Winfrey**[125]

If we are to find our way across troubled waters, we are better served by the company of those who have built bridges, who have moved beyond despair and inertia.
—**Marilyn Ferguson,**
The Aquarian Conspiracy[126]

We can always choose to perceive things differently. We can focus on what's wrong in our life, or we can focus on what's right.
—**Marianne Williamson**[127]

Everything can be taken from a man but one thing: the last of the human freedoms—to choose one's attitude in any given set of circumstances, to choose one's own way.
—**Viktor E. Frankl,**
Man's Search for Meaning[128]

The one thing you can't take away from me is the way I choose to respond to what you do to me. The last of one's freedoms is to choose one's attitude in any given circumstance.
—**Viktor E. Frankl**[129]

Dreams

Our deepest fear is not that we are inadequate. Our deepest fear is that we are powerful beyond measure. It is our light, not our darkness that most frightens us. We ask ourselves, "Who am I to be brilliant, gorgeous, talented, fabulous?" Actually, who are you not to be? You are a child of God. Your playing small does not serve the world. There is nothing enlightened about shrinking so that other people won't feel insecure around you. We are all meant to shine, as children do. We were born to make manifest the glory of God that is within us. It's not just in some of us; it's in everyone. And as we let our own light shine, we unconsciously give other people permission to do the same. As we are liberated from our own fear, our presence automatically liberates others.
—**Marianne Williamson,**
A Return to Love: Reflections on the Principles of "A Course in Miracles"[130]

Whatever you can do, or dream you can, begin it. Boldness has genius, power and magic in it.

—Goethe[131]

Joy is what happens to us when we allow ourselves to recognize how good things really are.

—Marianne Williamson[132]

Imagine yourself as a living house. God comes in to rebuild that house. At first, perhaps, you can understand what He is doing. He is getting the drains right and stopping the leaks in the roof and so on; you knew that those jobs needed doing and so you are not surprised. But presently He starts knocking the house about in a way that hurts abominably and does not seem to make any sense. What on earth is He up to? The explanation is that He is building quite a different house from the one you thought of—throwing out a new wing here, putting on an extra floor there, running up towers, making courtyards. You thought you were being made into a decent little cottage: but He is building a palace. He intends to come and live in it Himself.

—C. S. Lewis, *Mere Christianity*[133]

He who has a why to live for can bear almost any how.

— Friedrich Nietzsche[134]

I've come to believe that each of us has a personal calling that's as unique as a fingerprint—and that the best way to succeed is to discover what you love and then find a way to offer it to others in the form of service, working hard, and also allowing the energy of the universe to lead you.

—Oprah Winfrey[135]

Discovery and Interdependence

God has created several doors which open onto truth. He opens them to all those who knock on them with the hand of faith.

—Kahlil Gibran[136]

All have their worth and each contributes to the worth of the others.

—J. R. R. Tolkien, *The Silmarillion*[137]

Life doesn't make any sense without interdependence. We need each other, and the sooner we learn that, the better for us all.

—Erik H. Erikson[138]

I think if you are an intensely religious believer, as soon as you wake up, you thank God for another day. And you try to do God's will. For a nontheist like myself, but who is a Buddhist, as soon as I wake up, I remember Buddha's teaching: the importance of kindness and compassion, wishing something good for others, or at least to reduce their suffering. Then I remember that everything is interrelated, the teaching of interdependence. So then I set my intention for the day: that this day should be meaningful. Meaningful means, if possible, serve and help others. If not possible, then at least not to harm others. That's a meaningful day.

—Dalai Lama XIV,
The Book of Joy: Lasting Happiness in a Changing World[139]

Givers reject the notion that interdependence is weak. Givers are more likely to see interdependence as a source of strength, a way to harness the skills of multiple people for a greater good.

—Adam Grant[140]

My glorification of independence and individualism made me an easy target for the myth of meritocracy and overshadowed what in my heart I knew to be true: the deep interconnectedness I longed for with family, friends, colleagues, and even strangers is core to human survival. Interdependence is our lifeblood.

—Debby Irving,
Waking Up White: And Finding Myself in the Story of Race[141]

In the sweetness of friendship; let there be laughter and the sharing of pleasures. For in the dew of little things the heart finds its morning and is refreshed.

—Kahlil Gibran[142]

For Other Free Group or Individual Study Resources, Check Out:

lisauhrik.com
AmericaBecoming.com
franklincircles.org

Endnotes

Chapter 1

1.   Wikipedia contributors, "Cogito, Ergo Sum," Wikipedia, The Free Encyclopedia, accessed April 9, 2021, https://en.wikipedia.org/w/index.php?title=Cogito,_ergo_sum&oldid=1016799894.

2.   Yuval Levin, "Transparency Is Killing Congress," *The Atlantic*, February 9, 2020, https://www.theatlantic.com/ideas/archive/2020/02/lights-camera-congress/606199/.

3.   "'Free Bird,'" AZLyrics, accessed May 5, 2020, https://www.azlyrics.com/lyrics/lynyrdskynyrd/freebird.html.

4.   "Better Together," Genius, accessed May 24, 2021, https://genius.com/Jack-johnson-better-together-lyrics.

5.   Brendan Cole, "'Why Are You Doing This?' 'Because I'm Really Angry'—What Gilroy Shooting Suspect Said after Opening Fire, According to Witnesses," *Newsweek*, July 29, 2019, https://www.newsweek.com/gilroy-shooting-california-san-jose-1451502.

6.   "Anger Masks More Vulnerable Emotions," Mediate.com, March 4, 2016, https://www.mediate.com/articles/robertsR1.cfm.

7.   Jim Kloet, "A Special Place in the Brain for Swearing," Northwestern, February 18, 2013, http://helix.northwestern.edu/blog/2013/02/special-place-brain-swearing.

8.   Wikipedia contributors, "Junto (Club)," Wikipedia, The Free Encyclopedia, accessed April 2, 2021, https://en.wikipedia.org/w/index.php?title=Junto_(club)&oldid=1015656070.

9.   Andrew Marantz, "Benjamin Franklin Invented the Chat Room," *The New Yorker*, April 2, 2018, https://www.newyorker.com/magazine/2018/04/09/benjamin-franklin-invented-the-chat-room.

10.   "Junto Club," Benjamin Franklin Historical Society, accessed 2020, http://www.benjamin-franklin-history.org/junto-club/.

11. "Ben Franklin Circles," Ben Franklin Circles, accessed 2020, https:// benfranklincircles.org/.

12. "Ben Franklin Circles: Toolkit," Ben Franklin Circles, accessed 2020, https:// benfranklincircles.org/wp-content/uploads/Ben-Franklin-Circles-Toolkit-for-Hosts.pdf.

13. Carol Gilligan, *In a Different Voice: Psychological Theory and Women's Development* (London: Harvard University Press, 2016).

14. Stephen R. Covey, *The 7 Habits of Highly Effective People: Powerful Lessons in Personal Change*, 25th ed. (Simon & Schuster, 2013).

15. John Blakey, "Stephen Covey, Interdependence & the Deeper FACTS," Challenging Coaching, September 27, 2012, https://challengingcoaching.co.uk /stephen-covey-interdependence-the-deeper-facts/.

16. Blakey, "Steven Covey, Interdependence & the Deeper FACTS."

17. "Ben Franklin Circles."

Chapter 2

18. Zachary Siegel, "The Deadliest Year in the History of U.S. Drug Use," *New York*, December 23, 2020, https://nymag.com/intelligencer/2020/12/cdc-drug-overdose -deaths-in-2020-on-track-to-break-record.html.

19. Kendra Cherry, "Erik Erikson's Stages of Psychosocial Development," Verywell Mind, accessed 2020, https://www.verywellmind.com/erik-eriksons -stages-of-psychosocial-development-2795740.

Chapter 3

20. Cherry, "Erik Erikson's Stages of Psychosocial Development."

21. "A Majority of Young Adults in the U.S. Live with Their Parents for the First Time since the Great Depression," Pew Research Center, September 4, 2020, https://www.pewresearch.org/fact-tank/2020/09/04/a-majority-of-young-adults.

22. Maryam Mohsin, "10 Social Media Statistics You Need to Know in 2021," Oberlo, November 19, 2020, https://www.oberlo.com/blog/social -media-marketing-statistics.

23. Allison Sadlier, "Americans are streaming 8 hours a day during coronavirus lockdown," *New York Post*, April 14, 2020, https://nypost.com/2020/04/14/ average-american-streaming-content-8-hours-a-day-during-covid-19-according-to -new-research/.

24. Jaclyn Peiser, "Podcast Growth Is Popping in the U.S., Survey Shows," *The New York Times*, March 6, 2019, https://www.nytimes.com/2019/03/06/business/media /podcast-growth.html.

25. Scott Warren, *Generation Citizen: The Power of Youth in Our Politics* (Berkeley, CA: Counterpoint, 2019).

26. "More Young Adults Are Living at Home, and for Longer Stretches," Pew Research Center, May 5, 2017, https://www.pewresearch.org/fact-tank/2017/05/05/its -becoming-more-common-for-young-adults-to-live-at-home-and-for-longer- stretches/.

27. Bella DePaulo, *How We Live Now: Redefining Home and Family in the 21st Century* (Hillsboro, OR: Beyond Words Publishing, 2015).

28. "Welcome to the American Booksellers Association," American Booksellers Association, accessed 2020, https://www.bookweb.org/.

Chapter 4

29. Phillip C. Wankat and Frank Oreovicz, *Teaching Engineering* (New York: McGraw- Hill College, 1992), 264-283, https://engineering.purdue.edu/ChE/aboutus /publications/teaching_eng/chapter14.pdf.

30. Richard Fausset, "What We Know about the Shooting Death of Ahmaud Arbery," *The New York Times*, April 29, 2021, https://www.nytimes.com/article /ahmaud-arbery-shooting-georgia.html.

31. Evan Hill et al., "How George Floyd Was Killed in Police Custody," *The New York Times*, June 1, 2020, https://www.nytimes.com/2020/05/31/us/george-floyd -investigation.html.

Chapter 5

32. "2020 Small Business Profile," U.S. Small Business Administration Office of Advocacy, 2020, https://cdn.advocacy.sba.gov/wp-content/uploads /2020/06/04144224/2020-Small-Business-Economic-Profile-US.pdf.

33. "2019," U.S. Small Business Administration, accessed 2020, https://www.sba.gov /about-sba-navigation-structure/2019.

34. Lin-Manuel Miranda, *Hamilton: An American Musical (Original Broadway Cast Recording)*, Apple Music, accessed May 5, 2021, https://music.apple.com /us/album/hamilton-american-musical-original-broadway-cast -recording/1129446206.

35. "2019 Annual Report," New York Life, accessed 2020, https://www.newyorklife .com/assets/docs/pdfs/financial-info/2019/2019-Annual-Report.pdf.

36. T. R. Reid, *The United States of Europe: The New Superpower and the End of American Supremacy* (New York, NY: Penguin, 2005).

37. Amy Watson, "U.S. Newspaper Industry - Statistics & Facts," Statista, December 6, 2018, https://www.statista.com/topics/994/newspapers/.

Chapter 6

38. Sarah Stewart Holland and Beth A. Silvers, *I Think You're Wrong (But I'm Listening): A Guide to Grace-Filled Political Conversations* (Nashville, TN: Thomas Nelson, 2020).
39. James W. Fowler, *Stages of Faith: The Psychology of Human Development and the Quest for Meaning* (London: HarperCollins, 1989).
40. M. Scott Peck, *The Road Less Travelled: Special Edition*, 25th ed. (London: Rider, 2012).

Chapter 7

41. Wikipedia contributors, "Black Lives Matter," Wikipedia, The Free Encyclopedia, accessed January 17, 2021, https://en.wikipedia.org/w/index.php?title=Black_Lives_Matter&oldid=1021482848.
42. Wikipedia contributors, "Lady Mary Wortley Montagu," Wikipedia, The Free Encyclopedia, accessed January 17, 2021, https://en.wikipedia.org/w/index.php?title=Lady_Mary_Wortley_Montagu&oldid=1016036818.
43. Carina Storrs, "Hormones in Food: Should You Worry?," HuffPost, January 31, 2011, https://www.huffpost.com/entry/hormones-in-food-should-y_n_815385.

Chapter 8

44. Jean-Claude Bringuier, *Conversations with Jean Piaget*, trans. B. M. Gulati (Chicago, IL: University of Chicago Press, 1989).
45. Roger Aubrey, "Message to the Association," *Counselor Education and Supervision* 12, no. 4 (1973): 241–42.
46. Marcus Buckingham and Donald O. Clifton, *Now, Discover Your Strengths: How to Develop Your Talents and Those of the People You Manage* (New York, NY: Simon & Schuster, 2005).
47. Gallup, Inc, "CliftonStrengths Online Talent Assessment," Gallup, September 21, 2019, https://www.gallup.com/cliftonstrengths/en/252137/home.aspx?utm_source=bing&utm_medium=cpc&utm_campaign=new_strengths_ecommerce_brand_.
48. "Workkeys for Workforce Developers - National Career Readiness Certificate," Act, accessed 2020, https://www.act.org/content/act/en/products-and-services/workkeys-for-workforce-developers/ncrc.html.

49. Rebecca Lake, "Shocking Facts: 23 Statistics on Illiteracy in America," CreditDonkey, March 11, 2015, https://www.creditdonkey.com/illiteracy-in-america.html.

Chapter 9

50. Michael Commons, "Model of Hierarchical Complexity," Learning Theories, https://www.learning-theories.com/model-hierarchical-complexity.html.
51. Robert Kegan, *In Over Our Heads: The Mental Demands of Modern Life* (London: Harvard University Press, 1995).
52. Sally Carr, "Immunity to Change: How to Overcome It and Unlock Potential in Yourself and Your Organization," *Coaching: An International Journal of Theory Research and Practice* 2, no. 1 (2009): 86–88.
53. Angie Thomas, *The Hate U Give* (Balzer & Bray/Harper Teen, 2017).

Chapter 10

54. Pearl S. Buck, *The Good Earth* (New York, NY: Simon & Schuster, 2005).
55. Joseph Campbell, *The Hero with a Thousand Faces*, 3rd ed. (Novato, CA: New World Library, 2012).
56. Pádraig Ó Tuama, *Readings from the Book of Exile* (London: Canterbury Press Norwich, 2012).
57. Pádraig Ó Tuama, *In the Shelter: Finding a Home in the World* (London: Hodder & Stoughton, 2016).
58. Thomas Moore, *The Soul of Sex: Cultivating Life as an Act of Love* (New York, NY: HarperCollins, 1998).
59. Emily Dickinson, "Tell All the Truth but Tell It Slant — (1263)," Poetry Foundation, accessed 2020, https://www.poetryfoundation.org/poems/56824/tell-all-the-truth-but-tell-it-slant-1263.

Chapter 11

60. Wikipedia contributors, "September 11 Attacks," Wikipedia, The Free Encyclopedia, accessed January 19, 2021, https://en.wikipedia.org/w/index.php?title=September_11_attacks&oldid=1021345744.
61. Elisabeth Kübler-Ross and David Kessler, *On Grief and Grieving: Finding the Meaning of Grief Through the Five Stages of Loss* (London: Simon & Schuster, 2014).

62. Camelia Mihai, "SARAH– Emotional Response to Grief," Coaching & Therapy | Camelia Krupp, accessed 2020, https://cameliamihai.ch/wp-content/uploads/2016/07/SARAH-Emotional-response-to-grief.pdf.

63. Viktor E. Frankl, *Man's Search for Meaning* (Washington Square Press, 1985).

64. Wikipedia contributors, "David Attenborough," Wikipedia, The Free Encyclopedia, April 25, 2021, https://en.wikipedia.org/w/index.php?title=David_Attenborough&oldid=1019866986.

Chapter 12

65. "The Atlantic Books," *The Atlantic*, accessed 2020, https://www.theatlantic.com/ebooks/detail/jfk/.

66. "Home," The Sixth Floor Museum at Dealey Plaza, accessed 2020, https://www.jfk.org/.

67. Winston S. Churchill, *The World Crisis: 1911–1914* (RosettaBooks, 2013).

68. Norbert Juma, "70 John F. Kennedy Quotes on Life, Politics, and Greatness," Everyday Power, December 14, 2020, https://everydaypower.com/john-f-kennedy-quotes-jfk/.

69. "Three Early Childhood Development Principles to Improve Child Outcomes," Center on the Developing Child—Harvard University, October 6, 2017, https://developingchild.harvard.edu/resources/three-early-childhood-development-principles-improve-child-family-outcomes/.

70. "Evidence of Service Learning Benefits," SERC—Science Education Resource Center at Carleton College, accessed 2020, https://serc.carleton.edu/introgeo/service/benefits.html.

71. "NCSES Data," National Science Foundation, accessed 2020, https://www.nsf.gov/statistics/data.cfm.

72. "Lao Tzu: Quotes," Goodreads, accessed 2020, https://www.goodreads.com/author/quotes/2622245.Lao_Tzu.

73. T. S. Eliot, *Selected Essays, 1917-1932* (Houghton Mifflin, 2014).

Chapter 13

74. Peter Miller, *How to Wash the Dishes* (Boston, MA: Shambhala Publications, 2020).

75. R. T. France, *Gospel According to Matthew: Introduction and Commentary* (Nottingham, England: Inter-Varsity Press, 1985).

76. Langston Hughes, "Harlem," Poetry Foundation, accessed 2020, https://www.poetryfoundation.org/poems/46548/harlem.

77. "Langston Hughes: Poems 'Harlem' Summary and Analysis," GradeSaver, accessed May 11, 2021, https://www.gradesaver.com/langston-hughes-poems/study-guide /summary-harlem.

78. Susan Nolen-Hoeksema, *Women Who Think Too Much: How to Break Free of Overthinking and Reclaim Your Life* (New York, NY: Owl Books, 2004).

79. Nolen-Hoeksema, *Women Who Think Too Much*.

80. Nolen-Hoeksema, *Women Who Think Too Much*.

81. "The Neuroscience of Happiness," Greater Good Science Center, accessed 2020, https://greatergood.berkeley.edu/article/item/the_neuroscience_of_happiness.

82. Patricia Derrick, "Neurons That Fire Together Wire Together," Brainpaths, November 11, 2020, https://brainpaths.com/neurons-that-fire -together-wire-together/.

83. "The Secret Documentary," The Secret, May 13, 2020, https://www.thesecret.tv /the-secret-documentary/.

84. Cosmic Mama, "Home," The Law of Attraction, accessed 2020, https://loasecret .blogspot.com/.

Chapter 14

85. Genevieve K. Croft, "The U.S. Land-Grant University System: An Overview," Congressional Research Service, August 29, 2019, https://crsreports.congress .gov/product/pdf/R/R45897.

86. "Home," Livestrong.com, accessed 2020, https://www.livestrong.com/.

87. Warren E. Berkley, "Ecclesiastes 1:4-11 - There Is Nothing New Under The Sun," The Interactive Bible, August 2012, https://www.bible.ca/ef/expository -ecclesiastes-1-4-11.htm.

88. Dave Anderson, "A 'Declaration of Interdependence' Also Needed," *The Hill*, July 4, 2020, https://thehill.com/opinion/white-house/505856 -a-declaration-of-interdependence-also-needed.

89. "David C. Strubler Ph.D," *Psychology Today*, accessed 2020, https://www .psychologytoday.com/us/contributors/david-c-strubler-phd.

90. Steven Pinker, *Enlightenment Now: The Case for Reason, Science, Humanism, and Progress* (Harlow, England: Penguin Books, 2019).

Chapter 15

91. *Hamilton*, Disney+, accessed 2021, https://www.disneyplus.com/welcome/hamilton.

Companion Quotes for Group Topical Discussion:

92. PassItOn, accessed 2021, https://www.passiton.com/inspirational-quotes /5161-it-is-in-the-shelter-of-each-other-that-the.

93. "Gail Sheehy > Quotes," Goodreads, accessed 2021, https://www.goodreads.com /author/quotes/38338.Gail_Sheehy.

94. "Gail Sheehy > Quotes."

95. "C.S. Lewis > Quotes > Quotable Quote," Goodreads, accessed 2021, https://www .goodreads.com/quotes/1180-pain-insists-upon-being-attended-to-god-whispers- to-us.

96. "Oprah Winfrey Quotes," BrainyQuote, accessed 2021, https://www.brainyquote .com/quotes/oprah_winfrey_103803.

97. "Gail Sheehy > Quotes."

98. "Kahlil Gibran > Quotes > Quotable Quote," Goodreads, accessed 2021, https:// www.goodreads.com/quotes/11751-the-deeper-that-sorrow-carves-into-your -being-the-more-joy.

99. Quotefancy, accessed 2021, https://quotefancy.com/quote/15758/Oprah -Winfrey-You-get-to-know-who-you-really-are-in-a-crisis.

100. "Kahlil Gibran > Quotes > Quotable Quote," Goodreads, accessed 2021, https:// www.goodreads.com/quotes/3899-out-of-suffering-have-emerged-the-strongest- souls-the-most.

101. "Marianne Williamson > Quotes > Quotable Quote," Goodreads, accessed 2021, https://www.goodreads.com/quotes/18169-it-takes-courage-to-endure-the -sharp-pains-of-self-discovery.

102. "Viktor E. Frankl > Quotes > Quotable Quote," Goodreads, accessed 2021, https:// www.goodreads.com/quotes/132157-the-pessimist-resembles-a-man-who-observes -with-fear-and.

103. "Oprah Winfrey > Quotes > Quotable Quote," Goodreads, accessed 2021, https://www .goodreads.com/quotes/38079-i-trust-that-everything-happens-for-a-reason-even-if.

104. "A.A. Milne > Quotes > Quotable Quote," Goodreads, accessed 2021, https:// www.goodreads.com/quotes/391381-piglet-noticed-that-even-though-he-had-a -very-small.

105. "Kahlil Gibran > Quotes > Quotable Quote," Goodreads, accessed 2021, https://www .goodreads.com/quotes/34978-you-pray-in-your-distress-and-in-your-need-would.

106. Brené Brown, *What Separates Privilege from Entitlement Is Gratitude* (Independently Published, 2020).

107. Sanaya Roman, *Living with Joy: Keys to Personal Power and Spiritual Transformation* (Tiburon, CA: H J Kramer, 1986).

108. "Maya Angelou > Quotes > Quotable Quote," Goodreads, accessed 2021, https://www.goodreads.com/quotes/115604-let-gratitude-be-the-pillow-upon-which-you-kneel-to.

109. "Ray A. > Quotes > Quotable Quote," Goodreads, accessed 2021, https://www.goodreads.com/quotes/516390-saying-that-i-am-a-grateful-alcoholic-will-then-reflect.

110. "True Gratitude Quotes," Goodreads, accessed 2021, https://www.goodreads.com/quotes/tag/true-gratitude.

111. "Khalil Gibran Quotes (sic)," BrainyQuote, accessed 2021, https://www.brainyquote.com/quotes/khalil_gibran_110137.

112. "Kahlil Gibran > Quotes > Quotable Quote," Goodreads, accessed 2021, https://www.goodreads.com/quotes/67183-one-s-own-religion-is-after-all-a-matter-between-oneself.

113. "André Gide > Quotes > Quotable Quote," Goodreads, accessed 2021, https://www.goodreads.com/quotes/4661-man-cannot-discover-new-oceans-unless-he-has-the-courage.

114. "Ansel Adams > Quotes > Quotable Quote," Goodreads, accessed 2021, https://www.goodreads.com/quotes/69578-in-wisdom-gathered-over-time-i-have-found-that-every.

115. "Roman Payne > Quotes > Quotable Quote," Goodreads, accessed 2021, https://www.goodreads.com/quotes/1319447-a-person-does-not-grow-from-the-ground-like-a.

116. "Max Ernst > Quotes > Quotable Quote," Goodreads, accessed 2021, https://www.goodreads.com/quotes/732039-before-he-goes-into-the-water-a-diver-cannot-know.

117. "Jerry N. Uelsmann > Quotes > Quotable Quote," Goodreads, accessed 2021, https://www.goodreads.com/quotes/867108-the-camera-basically-is-a-license-to-explore.

118. "Jasleen Kaur Gumber > Quotes > Quotable Quote," Goodreads, accessed 2021, https://www.goodreads.com/quotes/7693442-not-all-doors-open-in-the-same-direction-and-with.

119. "Carol Burnett > Quotes > Quotable Quote," Goodreads, accessed 2021, https://www.goodreads.com/quotes/205215-only-i-can-change-my-life-no-one-can-do.

120. "Marianne Williamson > Quotes > Quotable Quote," Goodreads, accessed 2021, https://www.goodreads.com/quotes/692380-each-of-us-has-a-unique-part-to-play-in.

121. "Marianne Williamson > Quotes > Quotable Quote," Goodreads, accessed 2021, https://www.goodreads.com/quotes/149747-success-means-we-go-to-sleep-at-night-knowing-that.

122. "Marianne Williamson > Quotes > Quotable Quote," Goodreads, accessed 2021, https://www.goodreads.com/quotes/27273-in-every-community -there-is-work-to-be-done-in.

123. "Kahlil Gibran > Quotes > Quotable Quote," Goodreads, accessed 2021, https://www.goodreads.com/quotes/20271-you-give-but-little-when-you-give-of-your -possessions.

124. "Annie Dillard > Quotes > Quotable Quote," Goodreads, accessed 2021, https://www.goodreads.com/quotes/530337-how-we-spend-our-days-is-of-course-how-we.

125. "Oprah Winfrey > Quotes > Quotable Quote," Goodreads, accessed 2021, https://www.goodreads.com/quotes/34807-your-true-passion-should-feel-like-breathing -it-s-that-natural.

126. "Marilyn Ferguson Quotes," Goodreads, accessed 2021, https://www.goodreads .com/author/quotes/207146.Marilyn_Ferguson.

127. "Marianne Williamson > Quotes > Quotable Quote," Goodreads, accessed 2021, https://www.goodreads.com/quotes/246773-we-can-always-choose -to-perceive-things-differently-we-can.

128. "Viktor E. Frankl > Quotes > Quotable Quote," Goodreads, accessed 2021, https://www .goodreads.com/quotes/51356-everything-can-be-taken-from-a-man-but-one- thing.

129. "Viktor E. Frankl > Quotes > Quotable Quote," Goodreads, accessed 2021, https://www.goodreads.com/quotes/29837-the-one-thing-you-can-t-take-away-from-me-is.

130. "Marianne Williamson > Quotes > Quotable Quote," Goodreads, accessed 2021, https://www.goodreads.com/quotes/928-our-deepest-fear -is-not-that-we-are-inadequate-our.

131. "Johann Wolfgang von Goethe > Quotes > Quotable Quote," Goodreads, accessed 2021, https://www.goodreads.com/quotes/1028174-whatever-you-can -do-or-dream-you-can-begin-it.

132. "Marianne Williamson > Quotes > Quotable Quote," Goodreads, accessed 2021, https://www.goodreads.com/quotes/20300-joy-is-what-happens-to-us -when-we-allow-ourselves.

133. "C.S. Lewis > Quotes > Quotable Quote," Goodreads, accessed 2021, https://www .goodreads.com/quotes/13641-imagine-yourself-as-a-living-house-god-comes-in-to.

134. "Friedrich Nietzsche > Quotes > Quotable Quote," Goodreads, accessed 2021, https://www.goodreads.com/quotes/137-he-who-has-a-why-to-live-for-can-bear.

135. Quote Catalog, accessed 2021, https://quotecatalog.com/quote/oprah-winfrey -ive-come-to-be-baVZ6Wa.

136. "Kahlil Gibran > Quotes > Quotable Quote," Goodreads, accessed 2021, https://www.goodreads.com/quotes/197113-god-has-created-several-doors-which-open -onto-truth-he.

137. "J.R.R. Tolkien > Quotes > Quotable Quote," Goodreads, accessed 2021, https://www.goodreads.com/quotes/518504-all-have-their-worth-and-each-contributes-to-the-worth.

138. "Erik H. Erikson > Quotes > Quotable Quote," Goodreads, accessed 2021, https://www.goodreads.com/quotes/9853171-life-doesn-t-make-any-sense-without-interdependence-we-need-each.

139. "Dalai Lama XIV > Quotes > Quotable Quote," Goodreads, accessed 2021, https://www.goodreads.com/quotes/10277609-i-think-if-you-are-an-intensely-religious-believer-as.

140. "Prof. Adam Grant: Successful Leadership Styles Include Giving," National Center for the Middle Market, accessed 2021, https://www.middlemarketcenter.org/expert-perspectives/prof-adam-grant-successful-leadership-styles-include-giving.

141. "Debby Irving > Quotes > Quotable Quote," Goodreads, accessed 2021, https://www.goodreads.com/quotes/9126391-my-glorification-of-independence-and-individualism-made-me-and-easy.

142. "Kahlil Gibran > Quotes > Quotable Quote," Goodreads, accessed 2021, https://www.goodreads.com/quotes/3074-in-the-sweetness-of-friendship-let-there-be-laughter-and.

Acknowledgments

THIS BOOK IS a beautiful example of interdependence.

Thank you, Dave, for pushing me (kind of literally) into that group of unsuspecting publishers at the ABA meeting and for every navigational row since. Oars in the water, my Love.

Steve McCondichie asked those wise questions, then paired me with gifted and gentle editor Elizabeth Ferris. A blend of therapist, creative writer, and sage, she shaped this clay.

M. Harrison finds my foibles endearing and ideas interesting. Turns out, we're a pair that can pick up after a twenty-year hiatus and work on a book. (Or anything, for that matter.) She organized form and flavored substance with an equal measure of salt and pepper and cheered every time the book popped into her inbox. What a blessing.

Jennifer Watkins was the input queen who brought scintillating ideas at every step. She and Rick wondered if it would ever happen (but believed anyway). And here we are (in spite of ourselves).

Sharon Cochrane, seamless forever friend and reading ambassador, birthed the phrase "Declaration of Interdependence" and always appeared on cue, asking the toughest questions and bringing rich ideas.

Colleagues Joy Watkins and Brianna Patel added illustrations, and H. Kim Maxson contributed the delightful and helpful artwork that is used throughout. (Look, Kim—you're a published artist!)

To the developmental psychology professors at Peabody who fed this idea twenty-five years ago, to the independent booksellers and librarians that are clients and friends, to our little band at Franklin Fixtures that created the space for this to happen, to those I'm thankful to call family and friends, to all who live out the READ3 model (whether they know it or not) toward interdependence every day—gratitude.

And thank you, God—for life and love abundantly above anything I could ask for or imagine.

IF LISA UHRIK'S 17-year-old self were writing this bio, she would say it's about time. This was, after all, her "Pledge to America." Over 250 times, she stood behind a podium as a winner of the "My Pledge to America" VFW contest, passionately wearing her beloved blazers and promising that "America was not some idea etched in marble, but a living, breathing thing." She noted that while Lincoln and others had done their parts to create treasured freedoms, it was now "her turn" to contribute something. Her fifteen minutes of early fame led to multiple meetings with President Reagan and encounters with achievers like Chuck Yeager, William DeVries, and Marvin Minksy, and even an interview with reporter Helen Thomas. Lisa shared a piano bench with Ray Charles to sing "America" and then a mic with Lionel Richie to lead "We Are the World" in a small Denver ballroom. She asked J. Paul Getty what he did for a living and enthusiastically spilled a glass of water onto the King of Bavaria's plate. It turns out that 4-H-ers make for some serious citizens.

Lisa's been in a hurry since, at the age of four, she comprehended the brevity of this plane of existence. She's done developmental work in aerospace, led high-ropes events in Palm Desert, run an online news source (before that was a thing), gotten a couple of masters degrees at Vanderbilt and completed much of a PhD program in Community Literacy, served over 45 manufacturers as strategic and lean consultant, owned several small businesses, and run a strategic pay program in education (concluding that was a terrible idea).

With husband Dave, Lisa is co-owner of Franklin Fixtures, a small manufacturing company dedicated to making shelving systems and other millwork, improving literacy through independent bookstores and libraries, and building local talent through a sustainable maker model. She also spends time supporting independent artists, developing a peer-based mentorship program, and loving on four dogs and a large extended family that has adopted her.

Everyone thinks she's a little "extra," and she takes it as a compliment—because she's *that* extra. Organizational development expert, developmental psychologist, community-space thought leader, entrepreneur, manufacturing geek/strategist, and obsessive pattern-language enthusiast, her "why" hearkens back to that 4-H pledge. And she hopes this book inspires yours.

Also Available from Blissful Beings

Unconditioned Love by Staci Diffendaffer

Throwing It All Away by Nina Owen

Forthcoming from Blissful Beings in Fall 2021

Whispers in Wonderland by Alicia Izzo

CPSIA information can be obtained
at www.ICGtesting.com
Printed in the USA
JSHW021319110721
16708JS00003B/19